the Church in the World

CHARLES COLSON

WORD
BOOKS

WORD BOOKS
Nelson Word Ltd
Milton Keynes, England
WORD AUSTRALIA
Kilsyth, Australia
WORD COMMUNICATIONS LTD
Vancouver, B.C., Canada
STRUIK CHRISTIAN BOOKS (PTY) LTD
Cape Town, South Africa
JOINT DISTRIBUTORS SINGAPORE –
ALBY COMMERCIAL ENTERPRISES PTE LTD
and
CAMPUS CRUSADE, ASIA LTD
PHILIPPINE CAMPUS CRUSADE FOR CHRIST
Quezon City, Philippines
CHRISTIAN MARKETING NEW ZEALAND LTD
Havelock North, New Zealand
JENSCO LTD
Hong Kong
SALVATION BOOK CENTRE
Malaysia

ISBN 0-85009-681-2 (Australia 1-86258-347-1)

Unless otherwise indicated, Scripture quotations are from the New International Version (NIV), © 1973, 1978, 1984 by International Bible Society.
Other Scripture quotations are from the following sources:
The New American Standard Bible (NASB), © 1960, 1962, 1963, 1968, 1971, 1972, 1973, 1975, 1977 the Lockman Foundation.
The Authorised Version of the Bible (AV).

The quotations in the following studies are all used by permission.

Studies 1 – 3 from *The Body*, by Charles Colson, © 1992 Charles W. Colson. Nelson Word.
Study 4 from *Institutes of the Christian Religion*, by John Calvin, © 1960. Westminster Press.
Studies 5,6 from *The Body*, by Charles Colson, © 1992 Charles W. Colson. Nelson Word.
Study 7 from *Power from on High*, by Charles Finney, © Christian Literature Crusade.
Studies 8 – 13 from *The Body*, by Charles Colson, © 1992 Charles W. Colson. Nelson Word.
Study 14 from *Lectures on Calvinism*, by Abraham Kuyper, © 1981. Eerdmans.
Study 15 from *Great Quotes and Illustrations*, by George Sweeting, © 1985. Word Inc.
Studies 16 – 18 from *The Body*, by Charles Colson, © 1992 Charles W. Colson. Nelson Word.
Study 19 from *Luther's Works (Vol. 53)*, by J. Pelikan and H.T. Lehmann Eds. © Fortress Press.
Studies 20 – 23 from *The Body*, by Charles Colson, © 1992 Charles W. Colson. Nelson Word.
Study 24 from *Letters and Papers from Prison*, by Dietrich Bonhoeffer, © 1967. Eberhard Bethge Ed.
Study 25 from *A Severe Mercy*, by Sheldon Vanauken © 1977. Bantam Books.
Study 26 from *Evangelism The Next Ten Years*, by Sherwood Eliot Wirt Ed © 1978. Word Inc.
Studies 27,28 from *The Body*, by Charles Colson, © 1992 Charles W. Colson. Nelson Word.
Study 29 from *Out of the Saltshaker*, by Rebecca Manley Pippert, © 1979 Inter-varsity Christian Fellowship of the USA.
Studies 30, 31 from *The Body*, by Charles Colson, © 1992 Charles W. Colson. Nelson Word.

Created, designed and typeset by Frontier Publishing International Ltd., BN43 6RE, England. *Reproduced, printed and bound in Great Britain for* Nelson Word Ltd. *by* Ghyllprint Ltd., Heathfield.
94 95 96 97 / 10 9 8 7 6 5 4 3 2 1

Making the most of the studies ...

Welcome

Welcome to the Oasis study entitled *The Church in the World!* Many Christians think that Christianity is about 'Jesus and me'. But it's far more than that. Jesus' eyes are focused on building His church — a community of believers throughout the world and in local areas. This book will help you to understand the character of the church and encourage you to be involved in building it.

2 days equals 2 months

We suggest that you take two days to cover each study and therefore two months to complete the book. You might want to work through the material more quickly, but if you take your time you are likely to benefit more. We recommend that you use the New International Version of the Bible (post-1983 version). The important thing is not that you finish fast, but that you hear from God *en route*! So aim to learn well and steadily build the teaching into your life.

Be the people

The church isn't some little institution that man has invented. It's a new society of people whom God has chosen. The church belongs to Jesus. One day it will be His glorious bride for all eternity, but for now it's His instrument for reaching the world.

Charles Colson challenges us to be the people that God wants us to be. He encourages us to be united in the truth and to be devoted to the Word, fellowship, breaking of bread and prayer. He also warns us not to accommodate to our culture, but rather to be holy and to stand up for godly values wherever we are. He exhorts us to serve others, to be faithful witnesses and to have a healthy fear of God.

The three sections under the main text relate to the teaching material. You may be asked to consider some aspect of the Christian life, to write down an answer, or to do something practical. The questions have been designed to help you think about your understanding of the church. Let the Scripture verses inspire you in your walk with God.

Build a storehouse

The Bible says, 'Wise men store up knowledge' (Prov. 10:14), and Jesus underlines this when He calls us to '[bring] good things out of the good stored up in [our] heart' (Luke 6:45).

God wants to encourage and inform you through His Word. That's what the 'Food for thought' section is all about. It gives you the invaluable opportunity to hear direct from God and to store up what He says to you. **Please use a separate notebook** particularly for this section. Not only will it help you to crystallise your thoughts, but it will also be of tremendous reference value in the future.

As you study, refuse to let time pressurise you. Pray that God will speak to you personally and expect Him to do so. You may sometimes find that you're so enthralled by what He says to you that you're looking up many Scriptures which are not even suggested!

Finally, God bless you as you discover what it means to belong to His church.

Identity crisis

'You say, "I am rich; I
have acquired wealth
and do not need a
thing." But you do not
realise that you are
wretched, pitiful, poor,
blind and naked'
(Rev. 3:17).

W hat's the character of the church? Is it a
local congregation, a denomination, all
Christians worldwide? Does it include those
who watch services on TV, those who are
baptised as infants, those who have never been
baptised? And what is the church supposed to
do? Worship? Evangelise? Grow? Feed the
hungry? Elect politicians? Fight pornography?
Opinions are varied.

Unbelievers aren't expected to know much
about the church's identity or mission. But
when Christians undergo a widespread identity
crisis, we're in big trouble. Why? Because
confusion strips the church of its authority.

The hard truth is that we have substituted
an institutionalised religion for a life-changing
faith. For most of us the church is the building;
its ministries are the programmes; its mission
is to meet the needs of its parishioners; and its
servants are the professional clergy. Church
growth refers more to such things as location,
marketing, architecture, programmes and head
counts than to the maturity of the people.

When compared with previous generations of
believers, we seem among the most thoroughly
at peace with our culture, the least adept at

▓ To pray

Pray that God will give Christians
throughout the world a new
understanding of the character and
mission of the church.

Pray particularly for your local church
leaders in this respect.

▓ To meditate on

The church is central to God's plan.
'And God placed all things under his
feet and appointed him to be head
over everything for the church, which is
his body' (Eph. 1:22,23).
'His intent was that now, through the
church, the manifold wisdom of God
should be made known to the rulers
and authorities in the heavenly realms,
according to his eternal purpose which
he accomplished in Christ Jesus our
Lord' (Eph. 3:10,11).

transforming society and the most desperate for a meaningful faith. Our raison d'être is confused, our mission obscured and our existence as a people in jeopardy. Our leaders know this, but seem unable to do anything.

Many Christians focus on personal obedience to Christ, as if what matters is 'Jesus and me'. But Christianity is not a solitary belief system. History tells us that any genuine resurgence of Christianity depends on a reawakening and renewal of the people of God. There is no such thing as Christianity apart from the church.

Too often Christians want to rush off and organise anti-pornography or anti-abortion campaigns, work for criminal justice reform, clean up inner city neighbourhoods and defend religious liberty. These are all noble and worthy good works, but are doomed to failure unless they proceed from who we are as God's people.

We can't give what we do not have. We can't impart values we do not hold. We can't do until we are. To be the church — our highest calling — depends on our grasping the very character of the body of Christ on earth. Only then can we understand what it means to live as the people of God, serving Him in today's world.

▓ To consider

What is your current understanding of:

a) the character of the church?

_____

_____

b) the mission of the church?

_____

_____

▓ Food for thought

➤ The church desperately needs holy fear — the passion to please God more than our culture and community.

➤ Read the following verses and write down in a notebook what God does for those who fear Him.

Psalms 25:14; 31:19; 33:18,19; 34:7,9; 60:4; 61:5; 85:9; 103:11,17; 111:5; 115:11; 145:19; 147:11; Luke 1:50.

➤ What are the marks of someone who is living, in the fear of God? In the fear of men?

➤ Pray that God will help you to know what it means to fear Him.

One of our great allies at present is the Church itself. Do not misunderstand me. I do not mean the Church as we see her spread out through all time and space and rooted in eternity, terrible as an army with banners. That, I confess, is a spectacle which makes our boldest tempters uneasy. But fortunately it is quite invisible to these humans. (Screwtape, a senior devil, instructing a junior devil on how to tempt and trap humans.)
C.S. Lewis

Consumer church

'If anyone comes to me and does not hate his father and mother, his wife and children, his brothers and sisters — yes, even his own life — he cannot be my disciple. And anyone who does not carry his cross and follow me cannot be my disciple ... any of you who does not give up everything he has cannot be my disciple' (Luke 14:26,27,33).

The roots of the church's identity crisis are embedded in our consumer mentality. To many, the church is a retail outlet, faith a commodity. People change churches as readily as they change banks and supermarkets. Many are looking for a spiritual social club that does not influence what they believe or do. They are interested not in what the church stands for, but in the fulfilment it can deliver.

If people see religion as a commodity, then the church feels it has to furnish a competitive product. This is a gradual, almost unconscious process — a little rationalising here, a little rounding off there. Sadly, responding to consumerism has profound consequences.

It dilutes the message. Sin is unmentioned and the focus is on a God who helps His people. Jesus is no more than the friend who shows us how to find happiness and self-fulfilment.

It changes the character of the church. The church is transformed from a worshipping community into a comforting haven from life's pressures. It becomes preoccupied with fellowship and abandons the search for truth.

It can pervert the gospel. While the church should comfort the suffering, this is different

▓ To consider

Read 1 Peter 1:15,16.
How can people be holy?
Give some practical suggestions.

_____

_____

_____

_____

▓ To meditate on

God wants us to grow spiritually.
'Speaking the truth in love, we will in all things grow up into him who is the Head, that is, Christ' (Eph. 4:15).
'We ought always to thank God for you ... because your faith is growing more and more' (2 Thess. 1:3).
'Like newborn babies, crave pure spiritual milk, so that by it you may grow up in your salvation' (1 Pet. 2:2).
'Grow in the grace and knowledge of ... Jesus Christ' (2 Pet. 3:18).

from looking within to discover and heal our wounded psyche. Jesus taught that our hope is not in finding our true self, but in losing it. **It strips the church of its authority.** When the church preaches a feel-good gospel, it points people to inner peace rather than to the way they fall short. Then the church forfeits its authority to proclaim truth and loses its ability to call its members to account. The task of the church is to make people holy, not happy.

Cultural values have so captured the church that we equate success with size. If a church isn't growing, someone is at fault and the right marketing strategy must be found. Growth can be a sign of God's blessing and it isn't always wrong to construct appealing programmes to draw people into services. The trouble comes when we confuse technique with truth, and compromise the mission or the message.

What matters is not whether a church uses drama, contemporary music or squash courts, but whether it challenges people to be holy. If a church preaches a message intended to keep everyone in a state of perpetual bliss, its growth is man-made. Holiness and biblical faithfulness are the true measures of the church.

▓ Food for thought

➤ Read Revelation 3:14–22. In verse 18 Jesus describes a 'hot' church. Write down in a notebook what you think a 'church on fire' looks like.

➤ Write down in a notebook what the following terms refer to:

- gold refined in the fire (Ps. 19:7–10)

- become rich (1 Tim. 6:17,18)

- white clothes to wear (Eph. 4:17–24)

- salve to put on your eyes (Eph. 1:15–21).

➤ How might Jesus 'rebuke and discipline' (Rev. 3:19) lukewarm churches today?

▓ To pray

Pray that God will help the leaders of your local church to avoid consumerism.

Pray that God will give them wisdom and courage to lead the church according to His plans and not according to those of other people.

Pray that the focus of the church will be on holiness rather than happiness.

I didn't go to religion to make me happy. I always knew a bottle of Port would do that. If you want a religion to make you feel really comfortable, I certainly don't recommend Christianity.
C. S. Lewis

On this rock

'Who do you say I am?'
Simon Peter answered,
'You are the Christ, the
Son of the living God.'
Jesus replied, 'Blessed
are you, Simon son of
Jonah, for this was not
revealed to you by
man, but by my Father
in heaven. And I tell
you that you are Peter,
and on this rock I will
build my church, and
the gates of Hades will
not overcome it. I will
give you the keys of the
kingdom of heaven;
whatever you bind on
earth will be bound in
heaven, and whatever
you loose on earth will
be loosed in heaven'
(Matt. 16:15–19).

In response to Peter's confession, 'You are the Christ', Jesus said, 'On this rock I will build my church'. And He promised that church a vast amount of authority: 'the keys of the kingdom'. Here was His instrument on earth, and whatever was done in His will would have eternal significance. From Jesus' declaration we learn four crucial lessons about the church. **It is not a building.** In the New Testament no one says, 'Let's go to church.' *Ekklesia*, the Greek word translated 'church', refers not to a structure, but to a gathering of God's people. **It is more than a collection of people.** Christianity is far more than 'Jesus and me'. When Peter made his confession, Jesus didn't reply, 'Good, Peter. You're now saved and will have an abundant life. Be at peace.' He announced the church. Immediately we confess Christ, we become members of His church.

The church is no civic centre, social club, encounter group or Sunday meeting place. It is a new society, created for the salvation of a lost world, pointing to the Kingdom to come. This is why we speak of the body with its different parts, the community of the redeemed, the holy nation and royal priesthood.

▨ To consider

In what sense is the church to be a 'new community'?

_____

_____

What kind of commitment does this require of church members?

_____

_____

▨ To meditate on

God is anticipating a radiant church. 'Christ loved the church and gave himself up for her ... to present her to himself as a radiant church, without stain or wrinkle or any other blemish, but holy and blameless' (Eph. 5:25,27). 'He has reconciled you ... to present you holy in his sight, without blemish and free from accusation' (Col 1:22). 'I saw the Holy City ... prepared as a bride beautifully dressed for her husband' (Rev. 21:2).

It belongs to God. Church leaders often speak about 'my church'. And most congregational squabbles arise over precisely this point: who owns the church? How easily we are impressed with our own importance! How foolishly we seek our identity in church positions! Where were we when God created His church? We live, breathe and serve at His pleasure. It's absurd to think that God would let us control His instrument for the redemption of mankind.

It will triumph. Jesus promised, 'The gates of hell will not prevail against it.' This was both an assurance and a commission to His people. We will triumph over the forces of evil, but we mustn't sit back and wait for the final victory. God is calling us to be a holy people who will stand for righteousness and justice now. When the people of God understand this commission, the church becomes the church.

But how do we define this church? The word *ekklesia* doesn't help us because in the New Testament it describes God's people in local churches, in homes, as representatives and in the world. Only if we understand the church's comprehensive character can we ever hope to recapture God's vision for His people.

➢ Divide a sheet of paper into five columns and head the columns as follows:

- specific local church
- several local churches
- church in a home
- church representatives
- universal church.

➢ Read the following Scriptures and write each reference in the most appropriate column:

Acts 9:31; 11:22; 13:1; 14:23; 15:22; 15:41; 16:5; 20:17; Romans 16:1; 16:16; 1 Corinthians 1:2; 12:28; 16:19; 2 Corinthians 8:23; Galatians 1:2,13,22; Ephesians 1:22; 3:10; Philippians 3:6; Colossians 1:18,24; 4:15; 1 Thessalonians 1:1; 1 Timothy 3:15; Philemon v. 2; Hebrews 12:23.

➢ According to the New Testament, where do denominations fit in?

▓ To review

List wrong motivations for taking on a particular job?

_____

_____

What should be your motivation?

_____

In the light of your answers, review your current involvement (or lack of it) in your local church.

> He cannot have God for his father who does not have the church for his mother.
> *Augustine*

The character of the church

I kneel before the Father, from whom his whole family in heaven and on earth derives its name (Eph. 3:14,15).

There before me was a great multitude that no-one could count, from every nation, tribe, people and language, standing before the throne and in front of the Lamb (Rev. 7:9).

Let us not give up meeting together, as some are in the habit of doing (Heb. 10:25).

The church is essentially spiritual — created by God Himself and known only by Him. It is universal in that it comprises people from all races, backgrounds and countries. Christians are all part of 'one, holy, catholic, apostolic church' — the body of Christ in the world.

From the beginning God planned to manifest this body through confessing communities. The pattern emerged after Pentecost: believers were to gather in local groups. Baptism not only signified forgiveness of sin, but also inclusion into the visible church.

Every believer is automatically part of the universal church, but each needs to follow the biblical pattern and become part of a local congregation with all the accountability that implies. Unfortunately, many Christians drift around, going where their friends lead them or where the pastor preaches the best messages. They have no sense of roots or responsibility, and some never join a local church at all.

If the purpose of the church is to herald the Kingdom, the ultimate community, then the Christian life must be rooted in community too. A failure to understand this causes much of our identity crisis. To deal with this crisis, we

▓ To pray

Pray about any difficulties that there are in your local church.

Ask God to give your leaders great wisdom in the decisions that they have to make.

Pray for any people who are involved in these difficulties.

▓ To meditate on

The church belongs to God.
'Be shepherds of the church of God, which he bought with his own blood' (Acts 20:28).
'To the church of God in Corinth, to those sanctified in Christ' (1 Cor. 1:2).
'Do you despise the church of God?' (1 Cor. 11:22)
'For you have heard ... how intensely I persecuted the church of God and tried to destroy it' (Gal. 1:13).

must understand the need for the universal and the local to support each other.

When people are saved and come into the universal church, those involved with them should guide them not just into a Bible study or fellowship group, but into a local church. That local church mustn't hold an independent stance, jealously guarding its own views on doctrine or practice. It must feel and behave as a part of the church universal, standing for biblical truth.

Sadly, today's church isn't all neat and tidy. It exists in tension. On the one hand we have the church that God has created and intends for ultimate consummation. Then we have the present reality: little congregations, vast denominations, street-corner preachers and TV orators who promise miracles for money.

The 'church of fact' is always struggling to conform to the 'church of faith', and we must live in the tension. Admittedly, the pettiness and failures can be disheartening at times. But the imperfect 'church of fact' is still God's vehicle for proclaiming and demonstrating the truth. And His promise to build the church stands for eternity.

▓ Food for thought

➤ The following verses remind us that sheep are in the habit of wandering around:

Psalm 119:176; Isaiah 53:6; Jeremiah 50:6; Ezekiel 34:6; Zechariah 10:2; Matthew 9:36; 18:12,13.

➤ The following verses tell us that Jesus came not just to save individual sheep, but to join them together:

Ezekiel 34:11–16; Micah 2:12,13; Luke 15:3–7; John 10:1–16; 1 Peter 2:25.

➤ In a notebook, write down why 'Christian sheep' are better off in a flock than roaming around.

▓ To consider

Read Matthew 8:5–13. What would you say are the marks of someone who is 'under authority'?

_____

_____

Read Hebrews 13:17. Why is it important to be accountable?

_____

To whom are you accountable?

So highly does the Lord esteem the communion of His church that He considers everyone a traitor and apostate from religion who perversely withdraws himself from any Christian society which preserves the true ministry of the word and sacraments.
John Calvin

The sin of presumption

Many Christians believe that a conversion experience must fit a certain pattern. People must know exactly when they prayed 'the sinner's prayer' and 'accepted Christ'.

For me, that expectation poses no problem because I had a dramatic conversion. But for many believers, this isn't the case. They can't pinpoint a sudden awakening, although they have a genuine relationship with Christ.

I've been in countless crusades where people have 'responded' to the gospel message. They pray 'the sinner's prayer' and behave like Christians for a while, but eventually fall back into old ways. The fact is: they have 'made a decision' but have undergone no more than a 'human' conversion. There's a great difference.

So should we abandon all gospel tracts and banish the 'sinner's prayer'? Not at all. These are useful techniques for presenting the good news. But they are precisely that — techniques. They are not sacred steps to salvation. They are not reliable tools which assure that God will work in some pre-programmed way. They are not the exclusive door into the Kingdom.

God chooses how He overcomes our rebellion. Like the wind that blows through the

▨ To consider

How can we avoid empty confessions of faith in Christ?

_____

_____

_____

_____

▨ To meditate on

It's God who saves people.
'I, even I, am the LORD, and apart from me there is no saviour' (Isa. 43:11).
'Salvation is found in no-one else, for there is no other name ... by which we must be saved' (Acts 4:12).
'God was pleased ... to save those who believe' (1 Cor. 1:21).
'Christ Jesus came into the world to save sinners' (1 Tim. 1:15).
'Salvation belongs to our God ... and to the Lamb' (Rev. 7:10).

trees, He can neither be seen nor directed. He touches the heart — and that's the point — He does it. He convicts; He calls people to Himself and He knits them together in His body.

The belief, 'there's one method to become a Christian' is a sin of presumption. We presume that we know the mind of God and use human means to determine who is and who isn't secure in the faith, and hence in the church.

When we make our methods the 'norm', we naturally question the faith of those who don't conform to it. This presumption can make us judgemental, arrogant and loveless. Certainly, we must be discerning. Jesus said that His disciples would be known by their fruit, so the way people live is a good measure of whether they belong to Him. While it's our responsibility to gently challenge others when they don't appear to be living by the truth, we can't afford to write them off just because their experience of conversion doesn't match our formula.

Ultimately, the sin of presumption hardens hearts, divides the body and grieves the Lord. It sets Christian against Christian and causes us to forget whose church it really is. Nothing is more destructive in the church than disunity.

▧ Food for thought

➤ Three passages that describe how different individuals became Christians are:
Acts 9:1–19; 10:23–48 and 16:22–33.

➤ Read these passages and write down in a notebook how each situation is:

a) different.
b) the same.

▧ To do

How do you respond to people whose experiences of God don't fit your formula?

_____

_____

_____

Are you presumptuous, judgemental, arrogant or unloving towards such people?

If so, repent of your negative attitude.

I cannot tell why He, whom angels worship.
Should set his love upon the sons of men,
Or why, as Shepherd, He should seek the wanderers,
To bring them back they know not how or when.
W. Y. Fullerton

United we stand

Make every effort to keep the unity of the Spirit through the bond of peace. There is one body and one Spirit — just as you were called to one hope when you were called — one Lord, one faith, one baptism; one God and Father of all, who is over all and through all and in all (Eph. 4:3–6).

How do we get unity? In the universal church we don't achieve it by 'reducing all elements of faith to the lowest common denominator' (unity in almost nothing). We focus on the great truths that all Christians share, e.g. the deity of Christ, the atonement, the resurrection, the second coming, etc.

This formula suits the universal church, but not the local church where believers come together for discipleship and worship. Here we need doctrinal agreement if we are to be of one mind, engaging in mutual submission under the authority of our agreed governing structure. Any division in the local church destroys the ability to worship, and those who deny the fundamentals face discipline or even exclusion.

Once we've established the orthodox beliefs, there is room for doctrinal disagreement in the universal church. Historians tell us that there were many different emphases among the early church believers. But their love for each other was so great that they overcame persecution and won many to Christ. So how do we achieve this 'unity with diversity'?

First, we must repent of presumption. We cannot say there's an unchangeable formula for

▓ To pray

Pray that God will bless other local churches in your area and establish His Kingdom through their witness.

Ask Him to unite the universal church in the truth.

Pray that the Holy Spirit will lead you into the truth.

▓ To meditate on

God wants us to be united.
'May they be brought to complete unity to let the world know that you sent me' (John 17:23).
'I appeal to you, brothers, in the name of our Lord Jesus Christ, that all of you agree with one another so that there may be no divisions among you and that you may be perfectly united in mind and thought' (1 Cor. 1:10).
'Be encouraged in heart and united in love' (Col. 2:2).

entry into the Kingdom: 'the sinner's prayer'. And we shouldn't be quick to judge. Protestants have no right to declare, 'Catholics can't be Christians'. And Catholics can't say, 'People can't be saved apart from the Catholic Church'.

Second, we can build bridges to those of other traditions. One community in Ann Arbor, Michigan consists of 1,500 people — two thirds Catholic, one third Protestant. Each group maintains its own worship service, but in other respects they have developed a common life.

Third, we can co-operate for witness. Instead of squabbling with one another, we can unite to meet social needs. Wherever people do this, the witness is powerful.

Fourth, we can fight secularism together. Many moral issues confront society: the dignity of life, medical ethics, religious liberty, justice. God's people belong in the trenches together.

The early church, led by apostles who had lived with Christ, understood their Teacher's call to unity. It undergirded all they did. The church members were 'of one mind', loved one another and knew God's power and presence among them. When we unite and proclaim His Word, we can turn the world upside down.

▨ Food for thought

➢ Read Ephesians 2:14–22. What does this passage say that Christ has done for those who have received His message of peace?

➢ How are those who have received the message of peace through Christ related to one another (v. 19)?

➢ What does it mean to be 'built on the foundation of the apostles and prophets'?

➢ How are the members of the church to be 'joined together' and 'built together' in the church? (See also 1 Corinthians 12:4–7 and 1 Peter 4:10,11.)

▨ To consider

What kind of unity must we work for in the local church?

_____

_____

How can we maintain this kind of unity while allowing for diversity in the universal church?

It's about time for Christians who recite the creed and mean it to come together for fellowship and witness regardless of denominational identity.
J. I. Packer

The apostles' teaching

They devoted themselves to the apostles' teaching (Acts 2:42).

'Go and make disciples of all nations, baptising them in the name of the Father and of the Son and of the Holy Spirit, and teaching them to obey everything I have commanded you' (Matt. 28:19,20).

The Word of God lies at the heart of the church's mission. Jesus commands us to make and teach disciples. And when Luke describes the early church, he begins by listing the believers' devotion to the apostles' teaching. Throughout the centuries, all traditions have recognised the priority of the Word.

People often apply human yardsticks when they choose a pastor. They focus on things like education, eloquence, charisma, pastoral heart and administrative ability. But they completely miss the essential criterion: is this individual steeped in the Word, wholly committed to teach the truth, and called by God?

Above all else, a pastor must be faithful to God. When he preaches, he's speaking for the Lord — and that's a terrifying responsibility. Paul preached 'with much trembling' (1 Cor. 2:3). And most of God's Old Testament leaders shrank in fear, groping for excuses: 'I'm too young.' 'I can't speak well enough.' 'I have unclean lips.' When Luther preached, his knees knocked, and Spurgeon said, 'We tremble lest we should mistake or misinterpret the Word.'

Preachers are not meant to resemble self-important spiritual superstars who strut across

▩ To question

Read Acts 20:27.
What sort of biblical teaching is unpalatable in today's church?

_____

_____

_____

_____

▩ To meditate on

Love the Word and God will bless you.
'But the seed on good soil stands for those with a noble and good heart, who hear the word, retain it, and by persevering produce a crop' (Luke 8:15).
'Blessed ... are those who hear the word of God and obey it' (Luke 11:28).
'If you remain in me and my words remain in you, ask whatever you wish, and it will be given you' (John 15:7).

the stage with pride and overconfidence. They are not meant to pump themselves up with boldness and 'the courage to preach'. Instead, they should stand in holy awe, conscious of their own frailty, yet trusting solely in God's power to help them speak.

They don't preach a therapeutic gospel, but the whole counsel of God. While behaviour science can play an important role in helping people, it cannot replace the gospel. Therapy works from the outside in and is concerned with changing behaviour. The gospel operates from the inside out and focuses on changing character. Therapy gives us what we think we need; the gospel gives us what we really need.

The task of teaching involves not just the pastor, but all church leadership. It permeates every level of the church. We must do all we can to equip believers with an understanding of biblical doctrine and teach them how to put the truth into practice in their everyday lives.

When the church is true to biblical faith, it will be identifiable, among other things, by the preaching and teaching of the Word. Make no mistake. Failure to teach is a betrayal of the Great Commission. And that's dangerous.

▓ Food for thought

➢ Read Exodus chapters 3 and 4.

➢ Divide a page of your notebook in half. On the left, write down the reasons Moses gave why God shouldn't use him. On the right, write down what God said to encourage him.

➢ Why was God angry with Moses (4:14)?

➢ Is there any reason why you shouldn't do what God is calling you to do?

▓ To consider

Read John 5:41,44.
What are the marks of those who seek praise from:
a) men?

_____

_____

b) God?

_____

_____

Away with this milk and water preaching of the love of Christ that has no holiness or moral discrimination. Away with preaching a love of God that is not angry with sinners every day. Away with preaching a Christ not crucified for sin.
Charles Finney

Fellowship

Fellowship is the number one thing people look for in a church. Some Christians think of it in social terms. 'It's about being together for retreats or leisure activities,' they say. Some see it as 'meeting for church events'. And others say that it's about 'obeying your discipler with unyielding discipline'.

The Greek word for fellowship, means none of these. It describes a new community in which individuals willingly covenant to share things in common, to submit to each other and to be mutually supportive. It embraces God and man and involves commitment and obligations.

Fellowship is more than unconditional and sympathetic love. It is also tough love that pursues truth and righteousness. For most Christians, it's easier to support people than to hold them accountable. That may be because we haven't taught accountability, or because we simply don't want to offend people. But when we fail to confront wrong, we are not showing love. True fellowship demands accountability.

Accountability is a hollow concept unless it is enforced. Few people join a club and fail to keep the rules. Similarly, no one should expect to join a church (which involves a free decision)

■ **To consider**

Read Galatians 6:2. What do you think this command means?

_____

_____

What does it mean for you?

_____

_____

■ **To meditate on**

The early church confronted sin. 'Ananias, how is it that Satan has so filled your heart that you have lied to the Holy Spirit?' (Acts 5:3).
When Peter came to Antioch, I opposed him to his face, because he was clearly in the wrong (Gal. 2:11).
'Your heart is not right before God. Repent of this wickedness and pray to the Lord. Perhaps he will forgive you ... For I see that you are full of bitterness and captive to sin' (Acts 8:21–23).

and then refuse to accept its authority. So when the church imposes discipline, why is it charged with everything short of fascism?

We discipline not only to enforce orthodoxy, but to maintain righteous behaviour. Sermons on holy living are empty exercises unless the church is willing to back them up with action. When we fail to discipline, we weaken the church and the world laughs at us.

A woman in a church in America announced that she wanted a divorce. The elders spent hours counselling her, but she refused to break off her relationship with her lover and insisted on attending Sunday services. The elders were forced to tell her either to repent or withdraw from the church. If she refused to withdraw, she would be expelled. In anger, she withdrew.

The first century believers demonstrated true fellowship when they were of one heart, shared their possessions, cared for those in need, and with great power proclaimed the risen Christ. As the church expanded, this concept of one fellowship united them and became the essence of the church's character and power. Today, that kind of fellowship would produce what it did then — a mighty outpouring of God's grace.

▓ Food for thought

➤ Read 1 Corinthians 5. Describe more specifically the people mentioned in verse 11.

➤ How do you react to the idea that people like this should be isolated?

➤ Why does Paul say that this immoral man must be expelled from the church?

➤ How might those outside the church view such an action? How would you reply to them?

▓ To review

Read Proverbs 27:5,6 and review:

a) the way you handle sinful behaviour in others

_____

b) your willingness to be challenged about your sin

_____

c) the way you would go about confrontation.

_____

Discipline guards the purity of the church, preserves the church by removing evil, and provides severe but loving correction for one who is in danger of falling into perdition.
Greg Bahnsen

Breaking bread and prayer

They devoted themselves to ... the breaking of bread and to prayer (Acts 2:42).

'Go into all the world and preach the good news to all creation. Whoever believes and is baptised will be saved' (Mark. 16:15,16).

'This is my body, which is for you; do this in remembrance of me ... This cup is the new covenant in my blood; do this ... in remembrance of me' (1 Cor. 11:24).

A sacrament is an outward expression of our faith in what God has done in us. It is meaningful only insofar as it declares the reality of God's action through His Son, Jesus. Traditions may differ on the meaning of the various acts, but all agree that they are centred on Christ, and that the two we will discuss here are clearly commanded by the Lord.

Baptism. It's astonishing how many Christians totally disregard the biblical mandate to be baptised. Baptism is the external witness of the invisible reality. It is Jesus' command in the Great Commission, and it is the first sign of admission into the church. For many, the act requires immense courage because it may mean imprisonment or even death.

The Lord's Supper. The thought that Jesus has asked us to do anything to remember Him should fill us with awe. When we break bread together, we signify in a physical way, our oneness with Christ. For this reason, Scripture sets out three conditions.

First, because it is only for believers. If an unbeliever takes communion, he taunts God since this sacrament is the supreme signal of the inner work of grace in someone's life.

▓ To consider

In the New Testament, how were Christians baptised?

_____

Why were they baptised in this way? (Clues: Matt. 3:16; Rom. 6:3.)

_____

Pray for believers for whom baptism may mean imprisonment or death.

▓ To meditate on

We are called to fast and pray. 'When you fast, put oil on your head and wash your face, so that it will not be obvious to men that you are fasting' (Matt. 6:17). 'The time will come when the bridegroom will be taken from them; in those days they will fast' (Luke 5:35). 'While they were worshipping the Lord and fasting, the Holy Spirit said, "Set apart for me Barnabas and Saul"' (Acts 13:2).

Second, those breaking bread must be at peace with one another. Before participating, every believer should examine his or her heart and take whatever steps are necessary to be reconciled with fellow believers.

Third, believers mustn't treat communion lightly. Paul warns us that those who do this drink judgement on themselves (1 Cor. 11:29). Casual Christians should flee the table rather than trivialise the sacred.

Prayer. The early believers weren't only devoted to the sacraments, but also to prayer. We don't pray primarily to get something from God, but to affirm that He is worthy of our full obedience and reverence. The key to effective prayer isn't self-centredness, but God-centredness. And we worship God not because we want to be happy, but because He is worthy.

How do we assess a local church? We look beyond the visible to the supernatural. To what extent is it under the seal of the Holy Spirit? In the early church the Spirit appointed officers, distributed gifts, gave power, revealed Christ, equipped for service, and brought fellowship. A present day church that is under the seal of the Spirit will manifest these characteristics too.

▓ Food for thought

➤ Read the following verses and note the devotion that the early church had to prayer.

Acts 1:14; 4:23–31; 6:1–7; 8:14–17; 9:11–19,40–42; 10:9; 12:5–17; 13:1–3; 14:23; 16:25–35; 20:36; 21:5; 22:17; 28:7,8.

➤ Write down in a notebook the situations that prompted them to pray.

➤ Write down three specific requests that you would like God to answer in the next four weeks.

➤ Pray for them all every day for this time and expect God to respond to your prayers. Is God asking you to fast as well as pray?

▓ To question

Read 1 Corinthians 11:17–34.
How can you break bread in an 'unworthy manner' (v. 27)?

_____

_____

_____

If you are feeling 'weak or sick' (v. 30), check that the reason is physical rather than spiritual.

The world drinks to forget; the Christian drinks to remember.
Steve Brown

Church versus world

'I am ... the truth'
(John 14:6).

Jesus answered '... I
came into the world, to
testify to the truth.
Everyone on the side of
truth listens to me.'
'What is truth?' Pilate
asked (John 18:37,38).

Pilate wasn't really looking for an answer when he asked Jesus, 'What is truth?' Either he didn't understand or didn't accept what Jesus' reply meant. If he had, he would never have turned away.

Many Christians turn away too quickly from Christ's claim, 'I am the truth'. Some think He was speaking metaphorically, as He did when He said He was the way, the door, or the vine. But this is no metaphor. Others assume He was confirming that He truly was the Messiah. That may be so, but He was saying much more.

Truth can be defined as 'genuineness or veracity'. This means that something is true when we can vouch for it or prove it through physical examination. Certainly, Pilate could not have denied that Jesus truly was standing before him. But Jesus' never meant to inform Pilate of truths *about* Himself. He wanted Pilate to know that He was *the* truth.

'What is reality?' This has always been man's greatest quest. Today, under the influence of Eastern mysticism and secularism, he seeks meaning not in some ultimate point beyond himself, but from within. 'Unless you can prove something, it isn't true,' he says. But we can't

▓ To question

How does an understanding of Jesus' claim, 'I am the truth' affect our view of Christianity?

_____

_____

_____

_____

▓ To meditate on

Jesus is the ultimate source of meaning. 'By him all things were created: things in heaven and on earth, visible and invisible, whether thrones or powers or rulers or authorities; all things were created by him and for him. He is before all things, and in him all things hold together' (Col. 1:16,17).
'(God) has spoken to us by his Son ... through whom he made the universe. The Son ... (sustains) all things by his powerful word' (Heb. 1:2,3).

find out whether Christianity is the truth through physical examination because truth — ultimate reality — isn't limited to what we observe. It's embodied in God Himself.

When Moses asked God for His name, He replied, 'I AM WHO I AM' (Gen. 3:14). As creator, God is the source of authority and meaning. That's why the Jews identified Him by the words, 'I am' (Yahweh). No wonder Jesus was almost stoned when He told them, 'before Abraham was born, I am!' (John 8:58) He was claiming to be God.

If Pilate had thought about Jesus' statement, he would have realised that Jesus was saying: 'I'm not just one truth among many. I'm the ultimate reality, the source and framework for all that you can see, know and understand. I'm responsible for the universe, for your existence and for the order in which life exists.'

Christianity isn't some religious structure or social institution, nor is it a set of beliefs about the nature of reality. It rests on ultimate reality. People come into a personal relationship with Christ and form a new society which points to the coming Kingdom. This Kingdom is centred on the core of all meaning — the God who has revealed Himself in human history. The truth.

▓ Food for thought

➤ Read John 8:31–58. How many times does Jesus refer to His being/telling the truth in these verses?

➤ In a notebook, write down how you would recognise

a) unbelievers
b) believers

who 'have no room for (Jesus') word' (v. 37).

➤ Write down three of the devil's greatest lies

a) to unbelievers.
b) to believers.

➤ How can Christians avoid error?

▓ To consider

In the face of Jesus' claim, how would Pilate most likely have understood the idea of truth?

_____

_____

How did his understanding affect his decision?

_____

_____

The church is against the world, for the world.
Hartford Declaration

All we like sheep

You must no longer live as the Gentiles do, in the futility of their thinking. They are darkened in their understanding and separated from the life of God because of the ignorance that is in them due to the hardening of their hearts. Having lost all sensitivity, they have given themselves over to sensuality so as to indulge in every kind of impurity, with a continual lust for more (Eph. 4:17–19).

Chat shows like 'Donahue' and 'Oprah' are now today's window on so called reality. Their producers search frantically for the most bizarre and erotic subjects and guests, looking for anything that's depraved, melodramatic, tragic, and, above all, sensational.

When anyone in the audience dares to voice disgust or concern, he or she is considered 'behind the times' and ignored. The applause is reserved for those who declare, 'Well, if this is what you want, who are we to object?' That's the world's way: 'Do what's right for you and you're being faithful to whatever is true for you. No one else has the right to tell you what to do. You decide.'

These TV shows present people as insecure animals who drift through life seeking nothing more than the fulfilment of their biological urges, or their insatiable need for self-esteem. All topics carry equal weight, with no objective moral distinctions. What matters is not what people do, but whether they find it meaningful. This relentless drivel renders viewers incapable of distinguishing between what is important and what isn't. Hours of watching neuters their moral senses.

▓ To pray

Pray that Christians will stand up for truth in:

- chat shows
- the media
- places of education
- the government.

Pray for particular individuals that you know who are in positions of influence.

▓ To meditate on

Christians mustn't be led astray. 'I am afraid that just as Eve was deceived ... your minds may somehow be led astray from your sincere and pure devotion to Christ' (2 Cor. 11:3). 'Turn away from godless chatter and the opposing ideas of what is falsely called knowledge, which some have professed and in so doing have wandered from the faith' (1 Tim. 6:20,21). 'Dear children, do not let anyone lead you astray' (1 John 3:7).

These shows trivialise the human experience and distract from the great questions of life. No one stands up and asks, 'What's the meaning of all this? How does this affect us? Is it right? Does this promote the greater good? What is the truth?' Rather, people are encouraged to pursue whatever they want. Life has no higher purpose than individual gratification.

While the Donahueites are oblivious of truth, others attack the notion that it exists. Their views have taken hold. Most people now believe that truth is relative. In other words, there are no absolutes. What is right and wrong usually varies from one situation to another. The only stable virtue left is unbridled tolerance: the modern broad-mindedness which declares that all values are equally valid (except a value that claims allegiance to absolute truth). There are no absolutes except the absolute that there can be no absolutes.

This is a frightening prospect, for ideas have consequences. The views of life that engaged the intellectuals and influenced the masses have dramatically affected the currents of history. What we now know as recorded events are merely manifestations of these world views.

▓ Food for thought

➤ Read Leviticus 18:1–5, 24–30. Why shouldn't God's people do what they want?

➤ Read 2 Kings 17:7–41. If you were God, what would you do if you saw the church 'following the practices of the nations'?

➤ Work out how you would answer someone who said, 'There are no absolutes'.

▓ To consider

What effect does the trivialising of truth have on our society?

_____

_____

_____

_____

Modern man has both feet firmly planted in mid-air.
Francis Shaeffer

Lost in the cosmos

'My people have been lost sheep; their shepherds have led them astray and caused them to roam on the mountains. They wandered over mountain and hill and forgot their own resting place' (Jer. 50:6).

'The Son of Man came to seek and to save what was lost' (Luke 19:10).

Everyone has a general belief about what is true. It forms the basis for our values and determines how we behave. If we are going to defend Christianity effectively, we must know what our culture's prevailing world view is.

It is secular. The word, 'secular' means 'of this world'. It emphasises the here and now and exalts instant gratification. There's no thought for tomorrow, and no value in yesterday.

It is anti-historical. Our culture is cynical about objective truth. 'There's no meaning behind history, law or politics,' it says. 'What past authors wrote is irrelevant. What matters is what we think of what they said. We revise the past to conform to current values.'

If history has no meaning, the past has no relevance. We can't draw on its traditions or learn its lessons, and we don't owe it any debts. Yet a stable society is built on values and virtues that have been handed down to us from the past. Take away a society's history, and you remove what binds it together and undermine a faith which is based on historical fact.

It is naturalistic. Today's society discounts the supernatural. 'There's nothing beyond what we see and feel,' it says. 'The natural is supreme.'

▓ To pray

Think of six friends or relatives who are not Christians.

In the light of the prevailing world views mentioned above, consider what each of these six might believe.

Pray specifically for each one — asking God to dismantle his or her false belief system and reveal the truth.

▓ To meditate on

We must not follow the world.
'May I never boast except in the cross of our Lord Jesus Christ, through which the world has been crucified to me, and I to the world' (Gal. 6:14).
'Anyone who chooses to be a friend of the world becomes an enemy of God' (James 4:4).
'Do not love the world or anything in the world. If anyone loves the world, the love of the Father is not in him' (1 John 2:15).

Naturalism puts all creatures on the same level. Since humans come from nothing and are going nowhere, there's no basis for human dignity and no logical reason to believe that we are better than any other living thing.

It is utopian. 'We are our own masters,' says society. 'God is dead. We are basically good and therefore have the capacity to create our own brave new world. Things are bound to improve with education and human progress.'

This century we have seen amazing advances in knowledge, education and technology. We have also seen horror and evil of unimaginable proportions. If we're basically good, there's no explanation for the wrongs we do. So we deny them, or blame them on sickness or on others.

It is pragmatic. If there's no objective truth, how do we decide between two actions? We focus not on 'Is it right?' but on 'Does it work?' So if you don't want the baby, flush it away. If your marriage is failing, get out. If an inside deal will profit your business, go ahead.

Schaeffer once remarked that modern society was lost in the cosmos, like an abandoned space vessel spinning randomly through the universe without meaning or purpose.

▓ Food for thought

➤ Read 1 Corinthians 10:1–13. Look up the four incidents to which verses 7–10 refer:

Exodus 32:1–6
Numbers 25:1–18
Numbers 21:1–9
Numbers 14:26–38.

➤ Write down in your notebook how Christians can imitate the world's

• idolatry/pagan revelry
• sexual immorality
• testing of God
• grumbling attitude.

➤ How do you make decisions?

▓ To consider

In our lost society, what do you think confessing Christ as Lord involves?

_____

_____

_____

_____

Modern man is betting his life ... that there is no judgement and that there is no eternity.
R. C. Sproul

The pillar of truth

God's household ... is the church of the living God, the pillar and foundation of the truth' (1 Tim. 3:15).

W hen we confess that Jesus is Lord, we acknowledge His sovereignty over all creation. This means that we are responsible for asserting that rule — of proclaiming His truth to our weary and sceptical culture. To do this, we must understand what we believe and recover the fundamentals of the Christian faith.

If Jesus' claim, 'I am the truth' is the foundation of our faith, we must begin with a renewed commitment to the truth. We must be convinced that Scripture is inspired by God, authoritative and infallible. While theological fads come and go, we must cling to orthodox beliefs — even if the world considers us crazy.

We shouldn't be timid and defensive about what we believe. Some people think, 'the church will be relevant only when its leaders fix their doctrines by majority vote'. But truth isn't determined this way. It's true whether people believe it or not. We can change our rules and practices — our forms, but not our foundation. The church is authoritarian. It is ruled by Christ and built on His Word.

This Word offends modern minds because it challenges the belief that people are essentially good victims of corrupt social influences.

▨ **To pray**

Pray that God will give those who preach in your local church courage to confront people with their sin.

Pray specifically for well-known preachers — that they will not become so taken up with God's power to heal that they forget to challenge about sin.

Pray that God will give you boldness to share a gospel that offers people challenge as well as blessing.

▨ **To meditate on**

We base our teaching on the Bible. 'For what I received I passed on to you as of first importance: that Christ died for our sins according to the Scriptures, that he was buried, that he was raised on the third day according to the Scriptures' (1 Cor. 15:3,4). 'According to the Lord's own word, we tell you that we who are still alive, who are left till the coming of the Lord, will certainly not precede those who have fallen asleep' (1 Thess. 4:15).

Instead, it teaches that they are independent agents who make moral choices for which they must accept personal responsibility.

Businesses penetrate new markets by giving people what they want. Similarly, the church is tempted to offer pleasure, but in a spiritualised form: 'if you think the world can give you a high, wait until you see what God can do'. Let's be imaginative in the way that we relate to the unconverted, but let's not trifle with the truth which is neither comfortable nor pleasant.

Teaching truth involves confrontation. People don't know that they're sinners and it's our job to tell them. Certainly, we should be sensitive in the way that we challenge the individual, but challenge we must. Conviction must precede conversion. If we present the gospel without mentioning sin, we are offering our own brand of therapy. The object is not to make people able to live with themselves, but with God.

On the surface, unbelievers may not seem so different from us, but their beliefs are utterly in conflict with ours. The scandal is that we have allowed them to dominate our culture. We have failed to stand for truth, to defend and advance an intelligent Christian world view.

▓ Food for thought

➤ Read Acts 2:14–41. Go through this passage and write down in a notebook the great truths of the faith to which Peter referred.

➤ Where is the point of confrontation? What watered-down reply could Peter have given his hearers instead of verses 38–41?

➤ Next time you present the gospel message, gently but firmly point out the need for repentance of sin.

▓ To consider

What sort of things does the world say about the church?

_____

_____

How should Christians respond?

_____

_____

If everthing that is, exists for the sake of God, then the whole creation must give glory to God.
Abraham Kuyper

A biblical world view

The LORD God took the man and put him into the garden of Eden to cultivate it and keep it (Gen. 2:15 NASB).

G od told Adam to 'cultivate and keep' the garden. To 'cultivate' means to increase creation's bounty; to 'keep' means to guard. Adam was to protect the garden from anything that might jeopardise its reflection of God's goodness. The Fall didn't negate this mandate. It made it harder to obey. Christ's work on the cross will one day restore creation to its former glory. Until then, believers must persevere in tending the garden of a fallen world.

First, we must recognise that God's righteous rule extends to everything. We must stop measuring our activities by secular standards. Instead, we must evaluate all we do against the yardstick: is it consistent with a biblical view of life, and does it bring glory to God?

Second, we must defend our beliefs. When a discussion on some important political or social issue arises, many of us clam up. Either we assume that the Christian perspective will lose, or we haven't done our homework. We must equip ourselves to offer a reasoned, coherent, thoughtful defence of the biblical world view.

Third, we must actively contend for Christian truth in every area of life. Believers have been commanded to keep the garden, to ensure that

▓ To do

In a notebook write down how you could fight for truth in your home, community, workplace and church.

Begin to act on these ideas this week.

▓ To meditate on

We must guard against falsehood. 'Men will arise and distort the truth in order to draw away disciples after them. So be on your guard!' (Acts 20:30,31) 'Watch out for those who cause divisions and put obstacles in your way that are contrary to the teaching you have learned' (Rom. 16:17). 'Pay no attention to Jewish myths or to the commands of those who reject the truth' (Titus 1:14).

God's beauty in nature is maintained. For this reason, we should be ardent ecologists. We should also care for animals, because God gave us dominion over them. And we should be concerned for human life, because everyone is created in the image of God. If lives are at stake, we must take a stand against the world.

Governments can neither confer nor take away human rights, they are given by God. Thus, the church is a passionate defender of man's liberty and civil rights. We stand up for the oppressed in nations around the world. We zealously seek God's justice in prisons and in the judicial system. We celebrate the arts as creative expressions that bring glory to the Great Artist. We champion morality because it reflects God's just and unchanging nature. We defend education because the pursuit of truth is the purpose of learning. And we see work as good — something by which we glorify God.

Since no area of life is beyond the rule of God, the Christian world view embraces every arena of experience and opportunity. We must get our heads out of the secular sand and stop being intimidated by our culture. Only then will truth be heard above the chaos of modern life.

▓ To consider

How do we 'equip ourselves to offer a reasoned, coherent, thoughtful defence of the biblical world view'?

_____

_____

_____

_____

▓ Food for thought

➤ The following passages give good advice about how we must approach the battle for the truth.

➤ In a notebook, summarise the teaching of each.

Romans 12:1,2
Colossians 2:8
Colossians 3:6,17
2 Timothy 2:15
1 Peter 1:13
1 Peter 3:15
1 John 4:1–3.

➤ Consider how ready you are to engage in the battle to recover truth. What is God saying to you about this?

(Our call) is this: that in spite of all worldly opposition, God's holy ordinances shall be established again in the home, in the school and in the state for the good of the people; to carve as it were into the conscience of the nation the ordinances of the Lord, to which Bible and creation bear witness, until the nation pays homage again to God.
Abraham Kuyper

Church in captivity

They called them in again and commanded them not to speak or teach at all in the name of Jesus. But Peter and John replied, 'Judge for yourselves whether it is right in God's sight to obey you rather than God. For we cannot help speaking about what we have seen and heard' (Acts 4:18–20).

Few of us confront an obvious foe the way that the first century Christians did. The baddies then were easily identifiable: the Caesars, the Pilates, the fertility goddesses. The early church challenged those reigning powers head-on. But for us, the challenge to the Christian world view is far more subtle.

Maybe if someone intimidated us after the Sunday morning service we would understand the dangerous forces around us. But that's not the way it works. The voices of culture are smooth, personable and reasonable, and their subtlety increases the danger of compromise.

In the East the pressure to conform to the state came frontally and brutally. In the West we have ensnared ourselves in the coils of politics. Certainly, we must be involved with political issues, but we must never put our political agenda ahead of our primary calling.

That's what happened in the sixties when the mainline denominations joined the civil rights movement. Initially, the church was genuinely motivated by compassion for the poor, but it soon slipped too far into politics. It focused on churning out press releases, marching in anti-war protests and lobbying Congress, and it

▇ To do

Name a Bible character who stood up for God against someone in authority.

_____

What was the issue at stake?

_____

_____

Consider whether God wants you to protest about something that you have read, seen on TV, etc.

▇ To meditate on

The devil is subtle — so are his agents. 'Now the serpent was more crafty than any of the wild animals the LORD God had made' (Gen. 3:1).
'His speech is smooth as butter, yet war is in his heart; his words are more soothing than oil, yet they are drawn swords' (Ps. 55:21).
'Satan himself masquerades as an angel of light. It is not surprising, then, if his servants masquerade as servants of righteousness' (2 Cor. 11:14,15).

neglected the higher call to worship the Lord, preach the gospel and make disciples.

When Christianity became the official religion of Rome in the fourth century, the church attained social and political acceptance. People with half-hearted faith flocked to churches that could no longer disciple them. Soon the word 'Christian' became meaningless. And when the empire that sanctioned it collapsed, the church nearly went down too.

In the Middle Ages, the unholy alliance of church and state resulted in bloody crusades and scandalous inquisitions. And in our own day, one of the most inglorious examples can be found in the church's failure to stand solidly against Hitler during the 1930s.

The church must stand apart from the state. Independence from the culture gives the church its reforming capacity and enables it to point society to the truth. The church must be free to address issues biblically and to speak prophetically, regardless of who is in power.

Ironically, political flirtations and dalliances have threatened the church's independence in the West even more than the direct oppression of the Communists in the East.

▓ Food for thought

➤ Read Acts 4:1–31. In a notebook, write answers to the following questions:

- What was the cause of the problem?
- How did Peter refuse to be accommodating?
- What caused the members of the court to marvel?
- What is the significance of this for us today?
- What warning was given to the apostles?
- How did they respond?
- How did the people overcome their fear of the authorities?
- On what was their prayer based?
- How can we learn to stand up against the threats and intimidations of the surrounding culture?

▓ To consider

Write down the dictionary definition of 'politics'.

_____

_____

In what ways are evangelicals succumbing to the temptation of politics?

_____

_____

It is common place that the mind of modern man has been secularized ... But unfortunately the Christian mind has succumbed to the secular drift with a degree of weakness and nervelessness unmatched in Christian history.
Harry Blamires

Accommodating the culture

Another threat to the church's independence is the acceptance of cultural values and practices. While we must to some extent gear our evangelism to the culture of our audience, we must never confuse technique with truth. Times change; truth doesn't.

The cross has always offended; the church hasn't. It's slipped into accommodating the culture. Pastors smooth the edges off hard gospel sayings and fail to teach about sin and repentance. And in order to appear sensitive to people's feelings, some churches have changed the wording in their hymn books and liturgy to embrace a male/female God.

The issue here isn't feelings, it's truth. The feminist dialect hides a militant agenda. When Christians use the dialect, they signal that they are accepting the entire agenda and embracing an ideology that attacks biblical authority.

The militants are seeking not equality, but the elimination of all gender distinctions. They assault the Scriptural teaching about the role of men and women, the character of the family and the patriarchal character of God Himself.

Believers mustn't be intimidated. Certainly, we should make sure that our language is

▨ To consider

How do Christians experience pressure to conform to the culture and society around them?

_____

_____

_____

_____

▨ To meditate on

Christians must stand firm in the truth. 'Be on your guard; stand firm in the faith; be men of courage; be strong' (1 Cor. 16:13).
'Stand firm and hold to the teachings we passed on to you, whether by word of mouth or by letter' (2 Thess. 2:15).
'Stand firm in one spirit, contending as one man for the faith of the gospel without being frightened ... by those who oppose you' (Phil. 1:27,28).

loving and respectful. But we need not, in a headlong attempt to appear relevant, salute the god/goddess of political correctness.

Another area where the church has raced to embrace the latest trends is sexual morality. More and more churches — even evangelical ones — are rationalising away biblical fidelity and accommodating the culture. Thus sexual practices that were once seen as sins, are now considered perfectly acceptable.

We are fearful of appearing out of touch with the times. But if we don't defend the truth and fixed moral standards, who will? Certainly, our fellowship must be loving and attract those who hunger and thirst. But we must never forget that the early church did not explode because it was a comfortable haven for those weary of life's pressures, or because it accommodated the culture's values. The early believers turned the world upside down because they confessed that Jesus, not Caesar, was Lord. They didn't embrace the culture, they scandalised it.

The church will again be the church not when it's applauded for being politically correct or sexually liberated, but when it's absolutely committed to the truth.

▓ To review

What evidence is there of 'accommodation':

a) in the life of your church?

_____

_____

b) in your own life?

_____

_____

Here's the great evangelical disaster — the failure of the evangelical world to stand for truth as truth. There is only one word for this — namely, accommodation
Francis Schaeffer

Let justice roll on

'Maintain justice and
do what is right, for my
salvation is close at
hand and my
righteousness will soon
be revealed' (Isa. 56:1).

'But let justice roll on like
a river, righteousness
like a never-failing
stream!' (Amos 5:24)

Martin Luther was one of the most significant figures in history. So what motivated him to take such a bold stand for Christ in his day?

First, he found out that Christianity is not a creed, but ultimate reality in Christ. He was convinced that the Scriptures are God's true and authoritative Word and had no choice but to stand for it — even if it meant taking on the entire power structures of his day.

Second, he discovered the central theme of Scripture: the justice of God. He realised that 'the Hebrew word, *tsedeq* (justice) literally meant 'righteousness'. Through it God was declaring that people and social structures must conform to the standards of His justice.

Third, he believed that the Christian must see others through God's eyes and promote righteousness for the world, for the structures of society and for people. This belief led to the biblical world view which affects all of life.

Our age needs to embrace this view. Many Christian endeavours have divided into two camps: social activists and soul winners. Those seeking to correct injustices and meet human needs have been accused of abandoning the

▓ **To pray**

Pray for those who administer justice in our nation, e.g. the police force, judges, lawyers, solicitors.

Ask God to make them impartial in their judgements — convicting the guilty and releasing the innocent.

▓ **To meditate on**

God wants us to show justice to others. 'The righteous care about justice for the poor' (Prov. 29:7).
'Administer true justice; show mercy and compassion to one another. Do not oppress the widow or the fatherless, the alien or the poor. In your hearts do not think evil of each other' (Zech. 7:9,10).
'What does the LORD require of you? To act justly and to love mercy and to walk humbly with your God' (Mic. 6:8).

call to evangelise the lost. The soul winners are derided for being concerned only with altar calls and notches in their Bible belts.

When Christians fail to grasp the definition of justice, they slice the Scriptures in two. On one hand there's an angry Old Testament God who punishes those who disobey His laws. On the other, there's a New Testament God who has discarded His law and showers grace on everyone. How desperately the modern church needs to recapture the full biblical vision of justice! How much it needs to see the unity of biblical truth and its relevance to all of life!

Luther realised that God wanted people to reflect His justice in their relationships with Him and others. This vision for biblical justice shaped not only his own life, but launched a movement that swept across the continent. His work was less a radical new beginning than it was a re-formation — a return to the essence of what the church had been in its noble past.

But the Reformation was more than a cleansing of ecclesiastical structures. Nothing was left untouched: the arts, commerce, government and education all came under its powerful influence — as we shall see.

▓ Food for thought

➤ Read Exodus 23:1–9. Write down in a notebook:

- the different kinds of people who are most likely to be treated unjustly
- how people treat them unjustly.

➤ Pray that God will give you the ability to discern injustice whenever you watch the TV or read the newspaper.

➤ Check whether you are treating others with absolute justice.

▓ To consider

How could your local church be more involved in bringing justice to your community?

_____

_____

_____

Consider whether you are totally just in all your dealings with others.

(The pope) would do better to sell St Peter's and give the money to the poor folk who are being fleeced by the hawkers of indulgences. If the pope knew the exactions of these vendors, he would rather that St Peter's should lie in ashes than that it should be built out of the blood and hide of his sheep.
Martin Luther

Results of the Reformation

You ... are being built into a spiritual house to be a holy priesthood, offering spiritual sacrifices acceptable to God through Jesus Christ ... But you are a chosen people, a royal priesthood, a holy nation, a people belonging to God (1 Pet. 2:5,9).

(Jesus) loves us and has freed us from our sins by his blood, and has made us to be a kingdom and priests to serve his God and Father (Rev. 1:5,6).

The Reformation had a profound influence on Western history. Here we consider just a few examples of that influence.

Politics and Government. State and church had been united in an unholy alliance, each using the other for its own purposes. Thus the church could bring little reforming influence on culture. The Reformers wrenched free from the state and enabled the church to make a great difference in society's values and structures.

They changed the view of man in relation to the state. Luther advocated the priesthood of all believers — that all people were equal and had direct access to God. Since individual rights came from God, the state's power could not be absolute, nor could a ruler's 'divine' authority permit arbitrary rule. God was the supreme governor; the sovereign, His servant to uphold His law. This vision of justice eventually led to the abolition of the slave trade, the reform of values and the prevention of exploitation of children and workers in the mines and prisons.

Vocation. Luther's view of God's sovereignty rent the veil between the sacred and the secular. He reasoned that if God's creation was good, and if people were stewards of it, then all

■ **To pray**

Pray for places of education. For:

- values that are based on biblical truth
- Christian teachers/lecturers
- governors — wisdom in governing
- appointment of teachers/lecturers
- increase in parents' prayer groups
- witness of Christian children/students
- church input, e.g. youth work
- RE lessons, Christian Unions
- moral issues, e.g. sex, bullying, smoking
- breakthrough of the gospel

■ **To meditate on**

Christians are called to work hard. 'Always give yourselves fully to the work of the Lord, because you know that your labour in the Lord is not in vain' (1 Cor. 15:58).
'Serve wholeheartedly, as if you were serving the Lord, not men' (Eph. 6:7).
'Whatever you do, work at it with all your heart, as working for the Lord, not for men, since you know that you will receive an inheritance from the Lord as a reward' (Col. 3:23,24).

work was holy in character. People should discern their skills and use them fully, seeking excellence and shunning idleness. This high view of work later became known as the Protestant work ethic and led to the most vibrant and productive economy in all history.

Economics. The Reformers rebelled against the belief that working for profit was immoral. They said that work done to the glory of God meant successful commerce and profit. But along with this high view of work, they also demanded stewardship and social responsibility. Workers were encouraged to produce more than they needed so they could give to the less fortunate.

Education. The study of history and ancient languages was important to the Reformers. They encouraged people to look at the way history was unfolding and to see God at work behind it.

Luther wanted to end illiteracy so that people could be instructed in the Scriptures. He therefore advocated compulsory education for all children. The Reformation restored the university to the cultural leadership it had known in the thirteenth century and stimulated popular education throughout the West.

▓ Food for thought

➤ Read 2 Thessalonians 3:6–15. In a notebook, write down:

- the marks of someone who is idle
- why Christians are exhorted to keep away from those who are idle
- how you think that an unemployed person should spend his or her time
- the difference between a busy person and a busybody.

➤ Carefully consider whether you're becoming lazy in a particular area of your life. What might be the reason for this?

▓ To consider

Read Psalm 64:5–8; Proverbs 22:22,23; Jeremiah 17:10,11.
What does God say about those who engage in injustice and exploitation?

_____

_____

_____

_____

The task of the people of God is, as far as possible in a sinful society, to reclaim the cosmos for God's created purpose.
Carl F. H. Henry

More results

One generation will commend your works to another; they will tell of your mighty acts. They will speak of the glorious splendour of your majesty, and I will meditate on your wonderful works. They will tell of the power of your awesome works, and I will proclaim your great deeds. They will celebrate your abundant goodness and joyfully sing of your righteousness (Ps. 145:4–7).

The effects of the Reformation were also evident in the areas of science, art and the church.

Science. The spiritual awakening created a great hunger to understand the wonders of the universe. In Luther's time, science claimed no conflict with religion. Instead, the notion of an orderly universe provided a context for the development of science, and progress was made in a number of areas. Astronomy's views of the universe challenged medieval myths. The fields of botany, zoology and geology flourished. Musicians learnt the mathematics of harmony. People studied anatomy, metals, plants, inertia, polar magnetism, optics and acoustics, and their studies led to the invention of pendulum clocks, refractor telescopes and air pumps.

Art. The Reformers saw all art as a means to give glory to God and to reflect the goodness and beauty of His creation. Artists and architects alike were inspired in their work, Shakespeare dominated the world of literature and composers like Bach made a conscious effort to exalt the Lord. Luther considered music the noblest of the arts. He provided music and hymns for the common people, not

▓ To pray

Pray that God will draw scientists to Himself through their discoveries.

Pray that goodness will become more fashionable than destructiveness, e.g. excellence at work, wholesome films, greater concern for family life, etc.

Pray for present day 'indulgence' sellers, i.e. those who promise blessings for money. Ask God to give wisdom to those who might be taken in by them.

▓ To meditate on

We should glorify God in all we do. 'My lips will glorify you' (Ps. 63:3). 'I will ... glorify him with thanksgiving' (Ps. 69:30). 'Whether you eat or drink or whatever you do, do it all for the glory of God' (1 Cor. 10:31). 'Live such good lives among the pagans that, though they accuse you of doing wrong, they may see your good deeds and glorify God on the day he visits us' (1 Pet. 2:12).

just the priests, and reinstated a tradition that went back as far as the early believers singing in their house churches in Jerusalem.

Ecclesiastical. The Reformation brought theological reform throughout the church. It halted the corrupt sale of indulgences (which were supposed to reduce the buyer's time in purgatory), and focused on justification by faith. It also pointed out that the church was not an institution, but the people of God.

If Luther had not taken his bold stand, our modern world would look different. The church in his day was in captivity. His movement freed it and made it an instrument of justice. It also provided the greatest political, economic and cultural benefits ever for Western civilisation.

What would free today's church from its captivity? A renewed commitment to the truth; a forsaking of consumer religion; an equipping of believers with spiritual weapons; a healthy fear of God; an acknowledgement of His sovereignty over everything and a commitment to proclaim justice in society. We would need Luther's courage to stand against our culture for truth and righteousness. If we were a people like this, we would turn the world upside down.

▨ Food for thought

➤ Read Nehemiah chapters 1 and 2. Jerusalem was in ruins and in disgrace.

➤ If you looked round today's church, what would grieve you most about it? Write these things down in a notebook.

➤ Earnestly seek God about what you could do to restore the church, e.g. I could pray more fervently about it, disciple others, support church events more, be more vocal about moral issues, etc. Don't let these ideas stagnate.

▨ To consider

Read Acts 2:46,47.
How do you feel that you should be 'praising God'
a) in your corporate housegroup meetings?

_____

b) in your private devotional times?

_____

Seek God about what action He wants you to take.

Next to the word of God, music deserves the highest praise.
Martin Luther

Greater things than these

'I tell you the truth, anyone who has faith in me will do what I have been doing. He will do even greater things than these, because I am going to the Father' (John 14:12).

W hen Jesus told His disciples that they would be able to do greater things than He had done, they must have been amazed. They had seen Him heal, cast out demons and raise the dead. How could they do greater things? What was He talking about?

Consider the context. Jesus was poised between the conclusion of His earthly ministry and the beginning of His heavenly one. He had fulfilled God's plans on earth; now He was telling His disciples that when He returned to the Father, He would send the Holy Spirit to them so that they could continue His mission.

True to Christ's promise, the early disciples were empowered by the Spirit at Pentecost and began to fulfil His plans for His new earthly body. They proclaimed the gospel, baptised new believers and gathered them into communities. The church grew. Generations of Christians, gifted in a thousand ways and empowered by the same Spirit, invaded every arena of human life, country and human endeavour. Whereas Jesus was limited by one human body, the body of Christ today is made up of millions of human bodies stamped with His image. We can do far more together than He could alone.

▓ To consider

Where do you see individualism in the Scriptures?

_____

_____

_____

Ask someone who knows you well whether you have a teachable spirit.

▓ To meditate on

Togetherness is important.
'He prophesied that Jesus would die for the Jewish nation and ... for the scattered children of God, to bring them together and make them one' (John 11:51,52).
'All the believers used to meet together in Solomon's Colonnade' (Acts 5:12).
'And in him you too are being built together to become a dwelling in which God lives by his Spirit' (Eph. 2:22).

In the light of this, it is scandalous that so many believers today have such a low view of the church. They see Christianity as 'Jesus and me' or treat the church as a building or social centre. They flit from church to church, or don't associate with any at all. This low esteem reflects the depths of our biblical ignorance and the extent to which we have succumbed to the obsessive individualism of our modern culture.

While every believer belongs to the universal church, failure to cleave to a local church is failure to obey Christ. It is within the local church that we commit ourselves to intimate relationships with fellow believers and submit ourselves to accountability, responsibilities and duties. It is where our Christian character is shaped and our spiritual gifts developed and exercised. It is the family whose ties cannot be broken. It is the training camp that disciples and equips believers to be God's people.

If we don't grasp the corporate nature of Christianity, we miss the heart of Jesus' plan. We are God's people — one body with many parts — spread throughout every arena of life, twenty-four hours a day, seven days a week, doing even 'greater things' than Christ Himself.

▓ Food for thought

➤ There is security in listening to someone else's advice. Read Proverbs 12:15; 13:10; 19:20; 20:18. Read also 1 Kings 12:1–24.

➤ Why do you think Rehoboam rejected the advice of the elders?

➤ How do you know whether the advice you're given is good?

➤ Pray that God will give you discernment in all your decision-making.

▓ To review

Read Galatians 5:16–18. What does it mean to live/ be led by the Spirit?

_____

_____

Take time today to review the overall direction in which the Spirit is leading you.

What's God's greatest challenge to you? How are you responding to it?

The holiest moment of the church service is the moment when God's people — strengthened by preaching and sacrament — go out of the church door into the world to be the church. We don't go to church; we are the church.
Ernest Southcott

Equipping the saints

It was he who gave some to be apostles, some to be prophets, some to be evangelists, and some to be pastors and teachers, to prepare God's people for works of service, so that the body of Christ may be built up until we all reach unity in the faith ... and become mature, attaining to the whole measure of the fulness of Christ (Eph. 4:11–13).

The first Christians didn't set out to turn their world upside down. What they did flowed from who they were — a holy people. Their very presence invoked a power that no one could repress.

Our society looks at what people do, not at who they are. Christians rarely say, 'I joined this church because it has a holy character, and emphasises discipleship and training for ministry'. Yet if the church is Christ's presence in the world, its primary task must be to build holy character, disciple people to maturity and equip them to live out their faith.

The Great Commission is not a charge to individuals, but to the church, and it involves more than evangelism. While transformation begins at conversion, it doesn't end there. God wants to see His people growing in holiness, namely sanctification. The maturing of character takes a lifetime, and it's done through discipleship in the context of a local church.

God has given to the church leaders whose task is to equip the members to be the church in the world. The problem is that the laity often don't see it this way. They turn up each Sunday and passively watch the entertainment up

▨ To consider

Write down the areas in which a Christian needs to discipline himself.

_____

_____

_____

_____

▨ To meditate on

It's important to go through training. 'Endure hardship with us like a good soldier of Christ Jesus. No-one serving as a soldier gets involved in civilian affairs — he wants to please his commanding officer. Similarly, if anyone competes as an athlete, he does not receive the victor's crown unless he competes according to the rules. The hardworking farmer should be the first to receive a share of the crops' (2 Tim. 2:3–6).

front. They totally fail to understand that they should be absorbing the truth, applying it to their lives, and taking it into the marketplace.

There are parallels here with my military experience in Marine officers' basic training. For the first few weeks, we were put through death-defying obstacle courses. We learned to handle and clean a rifle, and to disassemble and reassemble it blindfolded. We memorised the Marine handbook of military rules and our hearts and minds were imprinted for ever with the meaning of discipline. We went on to the rifle range, small unit tactics and then field manoeuvres. All of this was simulated warfare, but no one treated it like a game.

This should be true of soldiers of the cross. Yet instead of being well-disciplined church members, many Christians act like reserve units whose real jobs occupy them during the week and who turn out for occasional drills or hang out in the officers' club on Sundays. Our Handbook tells us that the church is the basic school of training for all believers. We must take discipline seriously because we are in real warfare. And the battle is not just for flesh and blood; it is for eternal souls.

▓ Food for thought

➤ Read Ephesians 4:11–16. In a notebook, write down:

- your understanding of the ministry gifts in verse 11, i.e. what apostles do, etc. You may need to do some further research into this.
- the 'works of service' that you feel God wants you to do.

➤ Write down what these phrases mean:

'unity in the faith'
'knowledge of the Son'
'mature'
'whole measure of the fulness of Christ'

➤ What are the marks of someone who has responded positively to the maturing process (vv. 14–16)?

▓ To do

In what areas are you undisciplined? Write down your thoughts in a notebook.

Pray that God will help you overcome in these areas.

Work on one of them this week/month and make yourself accountable to someone.

Commit yourself to mastering the other areas by writing them in your diary at the times when you want to deal with them.

Training for battle

'Can a blind man lead a blind man? Will they not both fall into a pit? A student is not above his teacher, but everyone who is fully trained will be like his teacher' (Luke 6:39,40).

S ince a biblical world view embraces all of life, the church must equip its members for all of life. This begins with basics and moves on to building the mature character of a seasoned warrior. There are many creative ways to train God's people, and the service for which they are trained will vary according to the needs of the locality. Here we will touch on the training areas that should be a part of every church.

The church should teach its members the Word and historic Christian truth so that they can defend their faith and apply it in the world. Various groups produce discipleship material which can supplement Sunday ministry.

The church should equip its members to lead godly lives in the marketplace. Christians need to be informed about the biblical world view and be trained in how to live by it.

The church should equip its members to build strong marriages and families. We must insist on premarital counselling and provide a full range of services designed to strengthen family relationships.

The church should equip its members to 'train up their children in the way they should go'. We must teach parents how to raise their

▩ To consider

Pray for the teachers in your local church.

Ask God to help them to communicate truth that will affect the whole of life, e.g. children, parents, work, money, etc.

▩ To meditate on

Jesus looks for maturity.
'The seed that fell among thorns stands for those who hear, but ... do not mature' (Luke 8:14).
'Solid food is for the mature, who by constant use have trained themselves to distinguish good from evil ... Leave the elementary teachings about Christ and go on to maturity' (Heb. 5:14;6:1).
'Perseverance must finish its work so that you may be mature and complete, not lacking anything' (James 1:4).

Let this mind be in you

Let this mind be in you, which was also in Christ Jesus: Who, being in the form of God, thought it not robbery to be equal with God: But made himself of no reputation, and took upon him the form of a servant, and was made in the likeness of men: And being found in fashion as a man, he humbled himself, and became obedient unto death, even the death of the cross (Phil. 2:5–8 AV).

The world seeks fame; Jesus says that greatness comes through service. As King of the universe, He deserved great glory, but He came to us as a suffering servant who died on a cross. Like Him, we are not called to chase acclaim, but to pour ourselves out for others.

Mother Teresa does that. I saw her on TV one evening. Her arms were round two emaciated young men — advanced AIDS sufferers who had just been released from prison and were about to enter one of her homes. When a reporter demanded why we should care about criminals with AIDS, she explained that these young men had been created in God's image and deserved to know His love.

Although Mother Teresa doesn't lead a church, church leaders need to learn from her example of selfless service. Change begins when we all start taking a hard look at ourselves.

First, we must reassess our objectives. Is our goal to be the most powerful church in town, to get on TV and influence the community? These things may happen, but they should be the fruit of faithful service, not the overriding objective. The church should be a community that worships God and makes disciples who are children in the fear of the Lord, and to be discerning in educational issues. We must also help young people grow in Christian character.

The church should equip its members to fulfil their vocation. Since our work brings glory to God, we need to teach diligence, creativity, thrift and excellence. We should also provide vocational counselling.

The church should equip its members to be good stewards. We must deal with such issues as the economy, business ethics, budgeting, tithing, and getting out of debt.

The church should equip its members to be effective witnesses. We need to train believers to identify and use their evangelistic gifts.

The church should equip its members with specialised training that enables them to reach out to those with particular needs. Compassion ministries are tough, front-line work, and many churches have developed great programmes for training believers to do them well.

As Christians are equipped, they must remember that their model is Jesus Himself — a wrong attitude will nullify all they do. That's why the church's primary focus must always be on developing the character of its people.

▓ To consider

How might your local church identify more with those who need help?

_____

_____

_____

▓ To meditate on

Our goal must be to serve others. 'The kings of the Gentiles lord it over them; and those who exercise authority over them call themselves Benefactors. But you are not to be like that. Instead, the greatest among you should be like the youngest, and the one who rules like the one who serves ... I am among you as one who serves' (Luke 22:25–27). '(Jesus) poured water into a basin and began to wash his disciples' feet, drying them with the towel' (John 13:5).

▓ To list

List the ways in which your church equips its members.

_____

_____

_____

_____

▓ Food for thought

➤ Read Titus 2 and 3:1–11. Focus on the verses through which God is speaking to you.

➤ Write down in a notebook what He's saying.

➤ Memorise the verses.

Every member of the Body has the potential to be — and should be fed and led towards functioning as — a fully equipped agent of Jesus Christ, as His minister.
Jack Hayford

The pedestal complex

Herod, wearing his royal robes, sat on his throne and delivered a public address to the people. They shouted, 'This is the voice of a god, not of a man.' Immediately, because Herod did not give praise to God, an angel of the Lord struck him down, and he was eaten by worms and died (Acts 12:21–23).

Celebrities used to be admired for their achievements. Now they're famous simply because they receive attention. TV is largely responsible for this obsession. Just appearing on the box carries such status that it hardly matters what you say or do.

For many believers, watching Christian TV or videos has become a substitute for participation in the local church. Why get involved with all those troublesome people down the road when you can just sit and listen to smooth preaching or a nice moral film in your cosy front room?

The pedestal complex is rampant throughout the church. Too many pastors see themselves as leaders, not servants, and their followers eagerly reinforce their beliefs. The pastor enjoys the title 'Doctor' and the Sunday School teacher looks down on lesser souls. This self-important attitude can infect the whole church. It can have disastrous consequences.

First, exalting leaders encourages spiritual Lone Rangers. Once an enterprise is launched, jobs depend on it and so, apparently, does the spread of the gospel. The leader's followers feel obliged to do what he wants, and fail to make him accountable. As a result, he falls into sin.

Second, exalting leaders can cause burnout and moral failures. People expect church leaders to be flawless in every area of life. The leader who tries to live up to their unrealistic expectations can become deeply frustrated, exhausted and tempted into immorality.

Third, exalting leaders results in a distorted view of people's worth. Christians often pursue the rich or influential. They give the best places to the wealthy and well-dressed, and reserve the back seats for those who are 'unimportant'.

Fourth, exalting leaders distorts the theology of the church. The Christian leader who is constantly the object of adulation soon can't live without it. He then, often unconsciously, stops preaching challenging messages and begins speaking to gain praise.

Fifth, exalting leaders lets everyone else off the hook. People think, 'We pay our leaders to do our spiritual service for us. The better they perform, the more we pay'. But the church is not a bunch of observers. Everyone's involved.

Of course, it's biblical to respect those with spiritual authority in the church. But there's a difference between respect and adulation. We must never glorify man more than God.

▓ Food for thought

➤ Read Daniel chapter 4. In a notebook write down the answers to these questions:

- Why do people exalt themselves?
- Why does God delay before he humbles them?
- What is God's goal in humbling the proud?
- What did Nebuchadnezzar learn about God?

▓ To pray

Pray for:

- a willingness among famous Christians to be accountable for their actions
- believers who opt out of the local church in favour of Christian TV or good moral videos
- a proper respect for spiritual authority in the local church.

▓ To meditate on

We must glorify the Lord alone. 'Blessed be your glorious name, and may it be exalted above all blessing and praise. You alone are the LORD' (Neh. 9:5,6). 'Praise the name of the LORD, for his name alone is exalted' (Ps. 148:13). 'O LORD, our God ... your name alone do we honour' (Isa. 26:13). '(He is) far above all rule and authority, power and dominion, and every title that can be given' (Eph. 1:21).

▓ To consider

Read Romans 2:11 and James 2:1–13. How do Christians show favouritism today?

_____

_____

_____

_____

Carefully examine your heart to see if you're guilty of favouritism.

We have too many people who have p[...] of medals and no s[...]
Warren Wiersbe

growing in holiness. It can't fulfil these functions if its leaders and people don't serve.

Second, we must avoid the snares. Pastors must delegate responsibility and let others preach. They can also do little things to remind themselves of their role. One pastor, instead of reserving a 'senior pastor' parking space next to the church building, uses the overflow car park a mile away and takes the shuttle bus.

When the temptation of pride knocks, we must lock the door against it. How do we do that? The knock is usually very faint. The best protection is accountability. Since we all have blind spots, we must submit ourselves to those who can see the logs in our eyes.

Third, we must identify with those we help. General Booth told his missionaries, 'Go to the Indian as a brother, which indeed you are, and show the love which none can doubt you feel ... eat and drink and dress and live by his side. Speak his language, share his sorrow'.

Christians can only be truly Christian when they are willing to be emptied out for others. There are no harder words in all of Scripture than Jesus' command, 'Love each other as I have loved you' (John 15:12).

▓ Food for thought

➤ Read 1 Samuel 2:1–10 and Luke 1:46–55.

➤ Write down in a notebook what you learn about the Lord from these verses.

➤ What are the marks of someone who is humble before God?

▓ To respond

Read 1 Peter 4:10,11. How are you obeying this command?

_____

_____

_____

Is God challenging you to be more of a servant than you are now?

Ask Him what He wants you to do and do it.

The church is herself only when she exists for humanity ... She must take her part in the social life of the world, not lording it over men, but helping and serving them, She must tell men, whatever their calling, what it means to live in Christ, to exist for others.
Dietrich Bonhoeffer

You shall be my witnesses

'But you will receive power when the Holy Spirit comes on you; and you will be my witnesses in Jerusalem, and in all Judea and Samaria, and to the ends of the earth' (Acts 1:8).

Jesus calls us to be witnesses, not just to witness. Knowing this is both wonderfully liberating and very demanding. We realise that we don't have to assault people with our tracts, yet recognise that being Christ's witnesses involves words and actions.

At one extreme are those who say lots about God, but lack love, purity or hope. There's the office worker who does the shoddiest work, the man who cheats his customers and the pro-life activist who slanders women entering the abortion clinic. At the other extreme are those who earnestly live their faith but never speak about it. Others admire them for their goodness but never know where it comes from.

Our first calling is to be witnesses, but within that calling is the need to proclaim. All believers are commissioned to share the good news, although not all are gifted by God as evangelists — like Billy Graham. He has fervently, and humbly, preached the gospel to more than a hundred million people in over eighty countries.

Those of us who don't have a specific call to be evangelists are still responsible for telling others about Jesus. Even when we feel reluctant about this, it's important that we obey

▓ To do

Consider whether you share Jesus enough with those who are around you during the day.

Ask God to give you opportunities to speak about Him.

Take them.

▓ To meditate on

Witnesses speak about Jesus.
'Those who had been scattered preached the word wherever they went' (Acts 8:4).
'Men from Cyprus and Cyrene, went to Antioch and began to speak to Greeks ... telling them the good news about the Lord Jesus' (Acts 11:20).
'Always be prepared to give an answer to everyone who asks you to give the reason for the hope that you have' (1 Pet. 3:15).

the nudge of the Holy Spirit. I'm especially sensitive about this because that's how I came to Christ — through a man called Tom Phillips.

Tom is a shrewd executive and a strong Christian. He's also the type who feels uneasy about creating an atmosphere to share his faith. He really didn't want to talk to me, but God just wouldn't let him off the hook.

He was then president of Raytheon, one of the largest and most successful companies in America. I had recently left the White House and was planning to return to Raytheon as legal advisor. Tom was nervous about meeting me because of the Watergate controversy — association with me might hurt the company.

The night before our meeting, Tom prayed, 'God, make Chuck Colson go away', to which the Lord seemed to reply, 'No, you tell Chuck about me. He needs a friend'. God had chosen Tom to tell me about Jesus, and how eternally grateful I am that he obeyed!

Jesus' words in the Great Commission could be rendered, 'as you are going make disciples'. Evangelism isn't a set of techniques. It's a consequence of everyday holy living which flows naturally out of the healthy life of the church.

▓ Food for thought

➤ Read Psalm 71 and write down in a notebook how the Psalmist proposes to use his mouth to proclaim the Lord.

➤ What phrase is repeated in verses 8, 15 and 24?

➤ Look back over the last week and consider what God has done for you. Tell someone about this today or tomorrow.

▓ To pray

Pray that:

- God will raise up evangelists who will be able to train others in evangelism.

- God will challenge those who need to:
  look hard at their daily conduct
  start telling others about Jesus.

- You will be sensitive to the Holy Spirit when He prompts you to speak about the Lord.

The best argument for Christianity is Christians: their joy, their certainty, their completeness. But the strongest argument *against* Christianity is also Christians — when they are sombre and joyless, when they are self-righteous and smug in complacent consecration, when they are narrow and repressive, then Christianity dies a thousand deaths.
Sheldon Vanauken

Concerns for the church

Though I am free and belong to no man, I make myself a slave to everyone, to win as many as possible ... To those under the law I became like one under the law ... so as to win those under the law. To those not having the law I became like one not having the law ... so as to win those not having the law. To the weak I became weak, to win the weak. I have become all things to all men so that by all possible means I might save some
(1 Cor. 9:19–22).

I f the church is to be effective in evangelising today's world, there are a few critical concerns that we need to discuss.

First, we must recognise that we're in a post Christian era. The world denies the existence of absolute truth. So when people hear you share the gospel, they interpret it as your personal preference — 'OK for you, not for me'. Even sharing your testimony may have little effect.

Certainly, we should preach the truth and give personal testimonies. God will often use them to convict. But on a purely rational level, the secular person's mindset is a barrier to his understanding. If we want to reach today's society, we must overhaul the evangelistic techniques that were developed in the 1940s, 50s and 60s, and address the human condition at its point of felt need — conscience, guilt, dealing with others, or finding a purpose in life.

Second, we must be creative and sensitive. Although we don't want to play around with the historic Christian message, we can translate it into language that our society understands. This can be done through music, drama, dance, multimedia and video. It can also be done through sensitivity to an audience. Christianity

▓ To pray

Pray around the five areas mentioned in this study, i.e. ask God to help today's church to:

- address real needs
- be creative and sensitive
- be a worshipping community
- bring converts into the local church
- reach out into the community.

▓ To meditate on

We must be gentle with unbelievers. 'Let your gentleness be evident to all' (Phil. 4:5).
'The Lord's servant must not quarrel ... Those who oppose him he must gently instruct, in the hope that God will grant them repentance' (2 Tim. 2:24,25).
'Always be prepared to give an answer to everyone who asks you to give the reason for the hope that you have. But do this with gentleness and respect' (1 Pet. 3:15).

seems remote to prisoners, but they can relate to a man who died alongside two thieves.

Third, evangelism naturally follows worship and fellowship. Many church members see the worship service as their evangelistic outreach. The focus is on an altar call, not on enjoying God. True worship should lead to evangelism.

Fourth, evangelism should bring converts into the local church. If it doesn't, it risks being out of God's will. Baptism and discipleship must be done in the context of a local church. We are out for disciples, not scalps, and we must never give an invitation for salvation unless there's a follow-up mechanism in place.

Fifth, we must direct our evangelism to the unbeliever. It's easy to steal sheep from other churches and then boast about our successful evangelism. Though evangelism will sometimes touch people within a local church who have never been 'born again', as a norm we should be reaching out to the unsaved in our locality.

Evangelism must flow from worshipping, godly communities which present the gospel in language that society can understand. We must proclaim the good news; we must also live it — like candles that draw others to the true Light.

The fundamental objective of (Billy) Graham's follow-up programme was not merely to get a person to come forward and register a decision for Christ, but to help solidify that decision and insure that the individual became an integral part of a local congregation. There his Christian life would be nourished, and his spiritual gifts developed and employed ... Recognition must be paid to Graham's early discernment that the true object of evangelism, in the context of the Great Commission, is discipleship.
Waldron Scott

The light of the world

O ne of the Reebok advertisements declares: 'Life is short. Play hard.' It underlines a world view which says, 'This life is all there is, enjoy it.' Our commercials bear out this 'fun of the moment' philosophy. We see advertisements depicting tanned young people windsurfing or playing volleyball on the beach and then relaxing with a cool drink. How easy it is to be blinded by the bright lights of the world and fail to see that they mask a great darkness!

Light is one of the main themes of Scripture. At creation, God commanded, 'Let there be light'. And at the end of time we will be living in a glorious city where night no longer exists. Jesus claimed to be the 'Light of the world', and told His disciples to let their light shine before men — to do good works to glorify God.

The key thing about light is that it's seen best in the darkest places. Strike a match in a brightly lit room and it won't exactly cause a stir! But strike the match in the darkness, and every eye will be fixed on it.

Jesus said, 'You are the light', not, 'You must become the light'. His presence within us automatically makes us light. So as we come together we form communities of light which

▓ To pray

Pray that:

- Christians will not be captivated by the world's bright lights

- they will shine brightly where God has put them.

▓ To meditate on

The world is actually in darkness.
'We look for light, but all is darkness; for brightness, but we walk in deep shadows' (Isa. 59:9).
'See, darkness covers the earth and thick darkness is over the peoples' (Isa. 60:2).
'I am sending you to them to open their eyes and turn them from darkness to light' (Acts 26:17,18).
'Our struggle is ... against the powers of this dark world' (Eph. 6:12).

the world cannot help but see. From these communities we take the light of Christ's love to the needy and hurting places where the gospel flame is not already shining. That can be a Hollywood mansion or an inner-city drug den.

Annie, Linda and Judy work voluntarily in the Kentucky Correctional Institute for Women which houses about 340 inmates. They take Bible studies and support the women, most of whom have been abused, betrayed or put down by men for much of their lives. 'In prison you can sense the presence of evil in an almost tangible way,' says Linda. 'You can feel the heaviness of the battle for people's souls ... like a battle between darkness and light.'

Annie has learned a lot from her twelve years' voluntary service. She's prayed, wept and searched her Bible for answers to the needs of particular women, many of whom have become Christians. She's also trained and involved over 150 volunteers from local churches.

In 1991 she received an award for her work from President Bush — a heavy medallion with a candle on it. Annie doesn't need to wear it in order to be seen. People know she represents Jesus. They can see Him shining through her.

▓ Food for thought

➤ Read John 1:4–9. Why does the Bible describe Jesus in terms of light?

➤ Read John 3:19–21. How do evil people respond to the light? Who comes into the light?

➤ Read 1 John 1:5–7. In practical terms, how do people:

a) walk in the darkness?

b) walk in the light?

▓ To consider

Read Matthew 5:13–16. How will you know when your light-bearing is truly effective?

_____

_____

In practical terms, what would that look like?

_____

_____

Be of good comfort, Master Ridley, and play the man. We shall this day light such a candle, by God's grace, in England, as I trust shall never be put out.
Biship High Latimer to Nicholas Ridley as they were being burned at the stake in 1555

Shine, Jesus, shine!

In him was life, and that life was the light of men. The light shines in the darkness, but the darkness has not understood it (John 1:4,5).

As a child, Sherry Woods believed that God wanted her to help bring justice to inner city children. She now manages a learning centre — a ministry of a primarily black church in Washington DC.

The Shaw district is a tough place with its fair share of drugs, shootings and despair. But on Tuesday evenings, the church welcomes thirty neighbourhood kids and matches them with thirty Christian tutors. Many of the learning centre 'graduates' are now in college; some are even tutors themselves.

The kids can be involved in more than just the Tuesday training programme. Several times a year they do service projects. Gathered into groups by age, they are asked, 'What would you like to do to help others?'

One winter, a number of eleven and twelve year-old boys thought that they would collect blankets for the homeless. As the idea grew, the group decided to make up packed meals too — and to invite the homeless to come to the church building and help themselves. A boy called William frowned at this. 'Why should they have to come to us?' he asked. 'We should go to them.'

▓ To pray

Pray that God will show your local church leaders where and how He wants the church to be reaching out into the community.

Pray for Christians you know who are already involved in social action, e.g. among the homeless, prostitutes, prisoners, etc.

▓ To meditate on

We are called to be light in darkness. 'Keep your lamps burning' (Luke 12:35). 'You were once darkness, but now you are light in the Lord. Live as children of light ... Have nothing to do with the fruitless deeds of darkness, but rather expose them' (Eph. 5:8,11).
'Become blameless and pure, children of God without fault in a crooked and depraved generation, in which you shine like stars in the universe as you hold out the word of life' (Phil. 2:15,16).

They made dozens of sandwiches and, on a snowy night, piled into a van and visited the grates and doorways where the homeless people sleep. The next night Sherry quizzed one of the boys on what he had learned. 'Well,' he said, 'it's like this. Just as God loves us, and we know it because people showed us He does, well, the homeless people need to know that He loves them too. So we have to show them!'

Jesus' light shines on the other side of the country too. A church in Los Angeles is involved in many outreaches, one of which is run by two women, Beverley and Jackie. Every Saturday morning they pack food into Jackie's old car, drive to a needy neighbourhood and give it out to twenty or so different homes. By their actions, they demonstrate to those who feel helpless that the church has not forgotten.

'People aren't going to get real help unless we do it,' says Jackie. 'It's time for the church to regain its rightful place. We've got to stop being so comfortable, and we've got to come out and help our brothers and sisters in need! The church has got to be the community that sees people like Jesus did when He was on earth — so they can see Him today.'

▩ Food for thought

➤ Read Isaiah 58:6–14. In a notebook write down:

- the sort of people whom God wants us to reach

- modern examples of each category

- what God will do for those who give themselves to others.

➤ What do verses 13 and 14 mean for you?

▩ To consider

The great goal of social action is to point people to the Lord Jesus Christ. Do you do kind things for others but hide the fact that you're a Christian?

_____

_____

Consider how shiny your testimony is, i.e. are you friendly, forgiving, kind, helpful, encouraging, etc.

_____

_____

Shine, Jesus, shine,
Fill this land with the
Father's glory;
Blaze, Spirit, blaze,
Set our hearts on fire.
Flow, river, flow,
Flood the nations with
grace and mercy;
Send forth your word,
Lord, and let there be
light.
Graham Kendrick

❏ STUDY 29

The salt of the earth

'You are the salt of the earth. But if the salt loses its saltiness, how can it be made salty again? It is no longer good for anything, except to be thrown out and trampled by men' (Matt. 5:13).

When Jesus told his disciples, 'you are the light of the world' He also told them, 'you are the salt of the earth' (Matt. 5:13,14). Many of us lump these two images together to describe good works. But light and salt aren't projects, they're characteristics of God's people. So how are they different?

Light is visible. Wherever God's people bear witness in a darkened world, their light can't be hidden. Salt is not so obvious. In fact, when used properly, it isn't visible at all.

In the ancient world, salt was the only preservative available. Farmers would slaughter their animals, carve the meat and then rub raw mineral salt into it until the salt was dissolved. This principle of penetration also applied when salt was used as a seasoning.

Meat will decay if it is left exposed to the natural elements. Society will decay if it is left exposed to the elements of evil in this world. For this reason, Christians must be 'rubbed' into culture, penetrating every aspect of life and preserving and seasoning our society.

Saltiness is vital in our modern world. The 1980s demonstrated that confrontation doesn't usually work. Almost every time we've launched

▨ To pray

Pray that God will help Christians who are working behind enemy lines.

- that they might have opportunities to communicate biblical values

- that they might be given wisdom to share those values tactfully

- that they might gain great influence among those with whom they work.

▨ To meditate on

God never despises small things.
'But you, Bethlehem Ephrathah, though you are small among the clans of Judah, out of you will come for me one who will be ruler over Israel' (Mic. 5:2).
'A poor widow came and put in two very small copper coins' (Mark 12:42).
'Because you have been trustworthy in a very small matter, take charge of ten cities' (Luke 19:17).
'Here is a boy with five small barley loaves and two small fish' (John 6:9).

a frontal assault on an issue, we've lost. This doesn't mean that we shouldn't confront. We will often have to stand courageously against evil, fight repressive laws, expose immorality or debate ethics. But in general, we will be more effective when we penetrate behind the lines, influencing the culture from within.

When an army fights behind enemy lines, it doesn't move its forces *en masse*. Rather, it infiltrates small units to disrupt the enemy's communication and attack strategic targets. There are many ways Christians can do this.

One woman works as an assistant producer for a network news programme. Whenever possible, she slips believers onto the show. A Christian speech-writer for a cabinet officer seeks to bring biblical values into the speeches. A mother spends one day a week helping a teacher in a school. She has gained the respect of the teacher and has even influenced many of the decisions that he's made.

Think what a difference it would make if thousands of Christians were getting rubbed into our culture in similar ways. Individual victories may seem small, but collectively they make a great impact on a decaying world.

▓ Food for thought

➤ Read Daniel 1. In what specific ways will you refuse to defile yourself in your present situation? Write them in a notebook.

➤ How did God bless Daniel for his courageous stand?

➤ Read Daniel 3. What excuses do Christians give themselves for accommodating to the culture around them?

➤ Read Daniel 6. Why do you think that Daniel was so open about his faith in God? Is God saying something to you about this?

▓ To consider

How can Christians lose their saltiness?

_____

_____

_____

_____

Consider how you could be more salty in your current situation.

The rabbit-hole Christian remains insulated and isolated from the world when he is commanded to penetrate it. How can we be the salt of the earth if we never get out of the saltshaker? ... We are salt and light. We make a difference because we are different. And when we live before God as we truly are, he will change the world in which we live.
Rebecca Manley Pippert

Infiltrators

'Let us send men ahead to spy out the land for us and bring back a report about the route we are to take and the towns we will come to' (Deut. 1:22).

We are not unaware of (the devil's) schemes (2 Cor. 2:11).

If we want to be salty, we must know our culture and influence it in as imaginative a way as we can. Writers have been doing this for centuries, with the result that much of the classic literature of the past three hundred years contains Christian truth.

Christian singers and sportsmen have had a similar positive effect on society. Just after the Washington Redskins won the Super Bowl in 1992, I invited their coach, Joe Gibbs to come and talk to a group of inmates in a prison in Virginia. When he stood up to speak, the cheers, whistles and applause of five hundred prisoners rocked the building.

Here's how he addressed them: 'A lot of people would probably look at me and say "If I could just coach in the Super Bowl, I'd be happy and fulfilled". But I'm here to tell you, it takes something else besides money, position, football, power and fame. The vacuum can only be filled through a personal relationship with Jesus. Otherwise we'll spend the rest of our lives in a meaningless existence.' He had won the right to be heard — through infiltration. **We must see ourselves as ministers of the gospel.** We aren't church-goers. We're people

▓ To consider

How do you think Christians could encourage one another more?

_____

_____

_____

_____

Do something today to encourage someone.

▓ To meditate on

We need to encourage each other.
'Let us ... make every effort to do what leads to peace and to mutual edification' (Rom. 14:19).
'Each of us should please his neighbour for his good, to build him up' (Rom. 15:2).
'Encourage one another and build each other up' (1 Thess. 5:11).
'Encourage one another daily ... so that none of you may be hardened by sin's deceitfulness' (Heb. 3:13).

who are being equipped to serve effectively in our vocations and community. We seek to be salt wherever God places us, and to accomplish His preserving, flavouring purposes.

We must be willing to be uncomfortable. Our culture is bound to ridicule us and regard us as strange. That can be costly — but obedience often is. If the approval of Christ means more to us than the approval of others, we'll be willing to be perceived as odd now and then.

We must learn to support and encourage one another. As agents behind enemy lines, we must establish a network through which we can pass on information. We can learn a lot about the world through magazines on current affairs, but we must also equip one another with Christian perspectives on critical issues.

What we must do can be likened to the way the underground operated in Europe during the Nazi occupation in World War II. It had its own elaborate system of signals, maps, charts, methods of communication and command structure. Although a bit extreme, the parallel is useful as Christians determine how they will network with one another in a culture hostile to the open expression of Christian truth.

▓ To pray

Are you aware enough of things that are happening in society?

Today, pray about something that's in the national news, e.g. an election campaign, a pro-abortion march, the high unemployment level, etc.

Write down as much information on the topic as you can beforehand, i.e. from the TV, radio, newspaper so that you can pray intelligently about the subject.

▓ Food for thought

➢ Read Numbers 13:17–33. What place do you want to infiltrate for Jesus, e.g. school, neighbourhood, work?

➢ Pray about how you could do this. (God may simply want you to pray on your own, or He may ask you to gather a prayer group, hold a monthly coffee morning, take colleagues to the gym/pub, etc.)

➢ If God just wants you to pray on your own, make sure that you allocate time to do this each day/week.

➢ If God wants you to do more, pray before you act. Does He want another Christian to help you? Should this be on a six month's trial?

Lord, here I am. Use me however you want to.
Aaron Johnson

The fear of the Lord

Some wonderful things are happening in churches around the world, but we cannot escape a deepening sense of dismay over the church in the West. It often takes its cues and defines its role by the ways of the world. It accommodates a consumer-oriented culture that wants, above all else, to feel good. And it focuses on action at the expense of character, on doing rather than being.

There's nothing wrong with seeking to meet people's needs or creating programmes to do so. The church should provide an environment where unbelievers feel welcome. It should grow. But when programmes and growth become the central focus, the church is in danger of profaning her first love.

To 'profane' means to take the holy and make it common. It's not just about using God's name in vain. It's about forsaking our assemblies, or offering empty words of devotion when we do gather. It's about singing hymns devoid of meaning, letting our thoughts wander during corporate prayer, and gossiping. It's about treating God as some remote abstraction.

We do these things at our peril. For the church is not God's whim; it is His love for

▓ To do

Consider whether you are guilty of treating holy things in a casual way, e.g. in your worship, in your speech, in your service, etc.

If God reveals anything to you, repent and be diligent about change.

▓ To meditate on

Christians should fear the Lord.
'The church ... grew in numbers, living in the fear of the Lord' (Acts 9:31).
'God ... accepts men ... who fear him and do what is right' (Acts 10:34).
'We know what it is to fear the Lord' (2 Cor. 5:11).
'Continue to work out your salvation with fear and trembling (Phil. 2:12).
'Live your lives as strangers here in reverent fear' (1 Pet. 1:17).
'Fear God' (1 Pet. 2:17).